100 Pearls

A collection of advice, guidance, and
recommendations from the supreme religious
authority His Eminence Grand Ayatullah al-Sayyid
Ali al-Husseini al-Sistani

100 Pearls

A collection of advice, guidance, and recommendations from the supreme religious authority His Eminence Grand Ayatullah al-Sayyid Ali al-Husseini al-Sistani

To all believers, male and female, the youth, the teachers and students of religious studies, and the speakers and volunteers who serve the Hussaini mission

I.M.A.M.

IMAM MAHDI ASSOCIATION OF MARJAEYA

Imam Mahdi Association of Marjaeya, Dearborn,
MI 48124, www.imam-us.org
©2021 by Imam Mahdi Association of Marjaeya
All rights reserved. Published 2021.
Printed in the United States of America

ISBN-13: 978-0-9997877-8-6

Contents

Contents

Introduction

In the name of Allah, the Most Gracious,
the Most Merciful

Praise be to God, Lord of the worlds, and may God's
salutation be upon the best of His creation,
Muhammad and his pure progeny

God's prophets, messengers, their successors, especially the Ahl al-Bayt (p), and all of the pious and ascetic scholars who followed their path and adopted their way of living from the Noble Quran and the legacy of the righteous servants, have been tasked with guiding the people towards what essential learning, cultivation, purification, awareness and remembrance has been ordered by God. Thus, God both gives glad tidings and warns, "so that those who were to be destroyed would face destruction with a clear knowledge of the Truth and those who were to survive would also survive with a clear knowledge of the Truth."[1]

---

1. The Holy Quran 8:42. Unless otherwise noted, all Quranic quotes in this book are from the Muhammad Sarwar translation.

Introduction

In our time, one jurist stands out among the current scholars in carrying this torch of guidance, Grand Ayatullah Sayyid Ali al-Husseini al-Sistani (may God prolong his life). For over thirty years, he has been enlightening others with his invaluable injunctions and pearls of wisdom that inform decision making in a variety of circumstances, situations, and occasions. In addition, he has been providing concise advice and clear instructions to those who have the honor of visiting him and seeking answers to their questions, whether through his office, website, in the Friday sermons that convey his edicts, and even by other means. Along with the knowledge that is evident in his advice, his statements are also characterized by sublime spirituality, witnessed by all when he speaks with complete candor and without prior preparation. Indeed, words such as these embody the saying, 'What comes out of the heart enters the heart, and what is uttered by the tongue only reaches the ears."

With the culmination of this beautiful collection of advice and recommendations and the verification of their authenticity, specific selections were extracted, paraphrased, or summarized, and organized into this booklet because the believers have long requested a collection of such kernels of knowledge so it may be a source of enlightenment. Therefore, no effort or care has been spared to provide the content as it was conveyed by His Eminence because this is the least of what is required to fulfill a sacred trust. Moreover, the occasion and date of each statement, as issued, have been noted accordingly. Yet, if there are any errors or deficiencies – because perfection can only be attributed to God – it is requested, with appreciation and gratitude, that you provide your feedback so the appropriate corrections can be noted and included in future publications. Surely God motivates those with sincere intentions.

Religious Authority

In the Name of Allah, Most Gracious,
Most Merciful

**Not all believers have to become specialists in
religious learning. Why do not some people from
each group of believers seek to become specialists
in religious learning and, after completing their
studies, guide their group so that they will have
fear of God.²**

In order to help the believers and the reader
in general have a clear understanding, a brief
summary about the importance of the religious
authority (marjaeya) and its respective duty during the
time of Imam Mahdi's occultation is presented before
the collection of injunctions, pieces of advice and
recommendations of the Marja, His Eminence, Grand
Ayatullah Ali al-Husseini al-Sistani (may God prolong
his life).

The importance of religious authority in the time of occultation

The religious authority in the era of Imam al-Mahdi's
occultation represents the legal or *shari* extension of

---

2. The Holy Quran 9:122.

the imamate, which itself legitimately represents the prophethood in carrying God's message to humanity. Thus, it is not surprising that the status of the religious authority is sacred in the hearts of Muslims because they recognize the legitimacy of their acts of worship and worldly transactions through it, and the necessity of resorting to the jurists who are the trustees of religion and have met the conditions of deep piety, specialized knowledge in the tenets of faith, and jurisprudence for assuming this critical position. Hence, the importance of the religious authority in the school of the Twelver Shia Imami Muslims becomes clear and obvious.[3]

The Role of the Religious Authority in the Time of Occultation

The followers of Ahl al-Bayt (p) faced a great trial with serious consequences when the infallible Imam went into his occultation which continues to be a challenge till this day. Among the most important of these challenges is the concealment of Islamic rules and judgements received directly from the infallible because of which scholars must exert effort in deriving the laws [from the authentic sources], and unfortunately, has even resulted in people acting upon supposition. As such, this has led to a multiplicity of opinions and rulings (*fatwa*) and a lack of centralization in the de facto representation of the infallible. Thus, the number of jurists and rulings have multiplied, and naturally, have led to fragmentation and division among the

---

3. Sayyid Monir Al-Khabbaz, *Maalim al- Marjaiyyah al-Rashida*, p. 7.

believers, which has only added to their ordeal with one test after another, requiring constant patience and forbearance. Despite this issue, the religious authority in general, irrespective of which qualified jurist represents it, has a specific and established role during the time of occultation, which includes the following:

1. Issuing religious rulings (fatwa)

The jurist must express his jurisprudential opinion on the application of Islamic law for various issues that need to be clarified when believers turn to him. As the holy verse states, "Not all believers have to become specialists in religious learning. Why do not some people from each group of believers seek to become specialists in religious learning and, after completing their studies, guide their group so that they will have fear of God."[4] As such, his relevant qualifications and specialization are in Islamic doctrine and jurisprudence. Moreover, due to his immense fear of God, which prevents him from pursuing any base desires or whims (i.e., worldly temptation), the general public turn to him for guidance and verification to ensure that their worship and dealings are religiously correct and free of defect.[5] It is not appropriate (i.e., valid) for anyone other than the jurist who fulfills all of the necessary requirements to take upon himself this responsibility and issue religious rulings (fatwas). Therefore, jurists have been designated for the task of extracting and clarifying what God has commanded for the people,

---

4. The Holy Quran, 9:122.

5. The Holy Quran, 9:122.

just like the prophets and their successors. God Almighty says, "All the Messengers that We sent spoke the language of their people so that they could explain (their message to them). God guides or causes to go astray whomever He wants. He is Majestic and All-wise."[6]

2. The judiciary role

The jurist, with his religious and personal qualifications, plays the role of a judge if people approach him with their disputes and claims. His judgment must be enforced (i.e., acted upon), and it is not subject to appeal, nor can it be argued. It has been narrated that Imam al-Sadiq (p) was asked about what to do if two people had a conflict regarding a loan or inheritance. The Imam said, "Look for those among you who have narrated our traditions and have examined what we related as permissible (halal) and forbidden (haram), and knew our edicts. Then, accept him as the judge [to decide your case] because I have made him a judge over you. If he issues a judgement based on our standards, and thereafter, his verdict is not accepted, then the conflicting parties have belittled God's commands and disputed our judgment. And, the one who disputes us has disputed God, and they are on the verge of associating someone with God (*shirk*)."[7]

3. The role of authority (*wilayah*)

Wilayah means to take responsibility and guardianship over a matter. For example, a father fulfills his

---

6. The Holy Quran, 14:4.

7. Al-Kulayni, *Al-Kafi*, vol.7, p.412.

responsibilities towards his children and acts as their guardian in all their affairs. God says, "Only God, His Messenger, and the true believers who are steadfast in prayer and pay alms, while they kneel during prayer, are your guardians."[8] Therefore, the jurist who fulfills all of the necessary requirements has a role of guardianship over the believers, due to being the representative of the infallible Imam. It should be noted that there is a difference of opinion about the extent of this guardianship and its authority with some who limit it to certain matters while others consider it to be unrestricted. However, at the very least, it is unanimously agreed upon that the jurist has authority in important matters related to protecting lives, honor, blood, wealth, orphans, matters of divorce, preservation of public order and security, endowment funds, Islamic rights, and other matters.[9]

Priorities of the Religious Authority in the Time of Occultation

Based on the important role the religious authority plays in the time of Imam Mahdi's occultation, there are a set of priorities that the religious authority must attend to in order to preserve this entity and the accompanying trust and responsibilities. In the present time, the most important of these priorities are:

---

8. The Holy Quran, 5:55.

9. Sayyid Monir al-Khabbaz, *Maalim al-Marjaiyyah al-Rashida*, p.8.

1. Educating the seminary faculty

The importance of the religious authority and its respective role is primarily underscored by the presence of [and the need for] jurists. Jurisprudential acuity is only achieved after many years of studying, teaching, researching, discussing, and debating various religious topics within the seminary. Hence, it is necessary for the jurist to give his full attention to those measures that secure and strengthen the Islamic seminary and preserve its knowledge, teachers, and students so that its scholarly movement and perpetual yield of jurists remains uninterrupted, which is crucial because they have been assigned the responsibility of carrying the religion. It has been narrated that Imam Ali bin Musa al-Rida (p) said, "The jurist (faqih) is the one who imparts to others his goodness, saves them from their enemies, spreads God's bounty upon them, and becomes the intermediary by which they gain God's pleasure. And it is said to the jurist [on the Day of Judgement], 'O' you who have sheltered the orphans of the family of Muhammad (pbuh&hp), and the one who has been a guide for those who love and follow them, stand and intercede for anyone who has gained or learned from you." He does so and then enters Paradise with thousands of servants [of God] who either learned his knowledge, learned from those who learned from him, or those who learned from them, up until the Day of Judgement. Thus, witness how much he has earned in return for what he achieved between the worlds (i.e., this world and the next).[10]

---

10. Al-Tabarasi, *al-Ihtijaj*, vol.1, p.9.

2. Propagating the true religion

Presenting the true religion in its purest, unblemished, and most authentic form, which conforms to human nature in every way, is one of the most important priorities of the religious authority. This is achieved by utilizing various means of spreading knowledge and awareness, including efforts aimed at debunking suspicious claims [about Islam], refuting any attempts to slander the faith, and by supporting believers who are less firm [in their faith] and are in constant need of an authentic source that points out the truth to them.

It has been narrated from Imam al-Sadiq (p) that he has said, "The scholar must reveal and spread his knowledge if innovations appear, because if he does not, the light of faith will be plundered [by those who seek to corrupt it]."[11] The Imam also said "The scholars amongst our Shia are like stationed guards who protect against Satan and his minions who harbor hatred for the Ahl al-Bayt (p). They prevent them from targeting and assaulting Shia who are weak [in faith]. Therefore, those of our Shia who takes this upon themselves is better than those who fought the Romans, the Ottomans, and the Khazars a thousand and thousand times, because the former are protecting the religion of our lovers while the latter are only defending their bodies (i.e., personal interests)."[12]

---

11. Al-Tabarasi, *al-Ghayba*, vol.1, p.88.

12. Al-Tabrasi, *al-Ihtijaj*, vol.2, p.5.

3. Supervising the affairs and interests of Muslims

One of the priorities of the jurists who have assumed a position of authority is to monitor the condition and situation of Muslims, the state of their countries, their interests, and contending with those who wish evil upon Islam, the well-being of the Muslims, and their countries. As such, they assume the responsibility of providing advice, guidance, and direction in various social and political matters, and even have to resort to intervening and confronting if necessary, as was the case in the Iraqi constitution and elections.[13] Similar instances of when the religious authority took such positions and issued a ruling concerning the protection of Muslims, their interests, and their lands include the

13. A fatwa was issued on 20 of Rabi al-Akhir 1424 AH following the decision of the occupation forces to select and assign a permanent constitution for Iraq, which ended the temporary government and assigned a new, permanent government based on that constitution. When the religious authority noticed the seriousness of the situation and saw how this decision would legitimize putting the law of the country in the hands of foreigners, which in turn would allow for the confiscation of the rights and resources of the people of Iraq, it issued a famous fatwa on that day. That fatwa declared that this decision was not religiously permissible and emphasized that writing of the constitution should be undertaken by the Iraqis and must then be presented to the Iraqi people for ratification. See here for more information regarding what followed: www.sistani.org/arabic/archive/273

Tobacco Protest in 1890 in Iran[14], the Iraqi revolt of 1920[15], and the fight against ISIS in 2014 in Iraq[16].

---

14. In 1890, Nasir al-Din Shah signed an agreement to limit the Iranian tobacco trade to a British company for fifty years. Accordingly, the right to buy and sell tobacco and any related products was taken from the Iranian people, 20% of whom worked in that sector, and was given to Britain instead. The agreement faced overwhelming national opposition from religious scholars, who considered it a threat to their country's future independence. A number of scholars tried to persuade the Shah to reconsider the agreement, but to no avail. So, the scholars, led by Sayyid Jamal al-Din al-Afghani, went to the great religious authority of the time, Mirza Muhammad Hassan al-Shirazi, who was residing in Samarra, and explained the matter to him to find a solution. Ayatollah Shaykh al-Shirazi initially sent several letters to the Shah asking him to cancel the agreement and stop its continuation, but the Shah rejected these demands. When Shaykh al-Shirazi gave up on convincing the Shah, he issued his famous fatwa and prohibited tobacco, stating, "In the name of God, the Most Gracious, the Most Merciful: today, the use of tobacco in any way is considered a form of fighting the Imam of our time, may God hasten his reappearance". The Iranians adhered to the fatwa and destroyed all ways of consuming tobacco, such as hookahs and other ways of using it. Moreover, all the tobacco shops closed. When the Shah failed to keep his deal and achieve his objective, which led to violence and aggression, the Shah was forced to annul the agreement with the British company after paying a fine of half a million gold liras.

15. After months of British occupation of Iraq and the escalation of the people's resistance in many areas of Iraq, especially Baghdad, the revolutionaries were joined by a large number of scholars and great jurists. They united and convened a historic meeting on the night of the middle of Sha'ban 1338 AH (April 21, 1920 CE) in the presence and under the leadership of the religious authority Ayatollah Shaykh Mirza al-Shirazi. He blessed their efforts and authorized them to fight to defend the country and the people, advising them to protect them, their wealth, and the honor of all sects and ethnicities alike. The people's revolution set

4. Preserving the Islamic seminary's autonomy

Maintaining the Islamic Seminary's independence in [religious] decision-making and ensuring its immunity from the influence of any government or external authority, no matter the pressure and threat, is another priority of the religious authority. During the period of occultation, the trustworthy jurists have been subjected to various types of constraint, abuse, displacement, exile, prison, torture, humiliation, and

---

out to fight the British forces and severely defeated them. The British had to surrender and give up to the existing government of Iraq that ruled. The strange thing is that Shaykh Shirazi passed away on the thirteenth of Dhul-Hijjah of the same year as a result of being poisoned. He was buried in Karbala, but the people were stunned and confused.

16. Following the terrorist ISIS invasion of the city of Mosul and occupation of vast areas in western Iraq, the religious authority in Najaf, representing Sayyid al-Sistani, confronted the situation and issued a famous fatwa, which was announced during the Friday prayer sermon in the Holy Shrine of Imam Hussain (p) in Karbala by his representative on the 5th of Sha'ban 14 AH. The fatwa stated, "The nature of the situation and the dangers facing Iraq and its people at the present time requires defending the country, its people, and the honor of its citizens. This defense is considered an obligation upon a sufficient number of citizens as is needed to fulfill the task (*wajib kifai*). Hence, the citizens who are able to pick up arms and fight the terrorists in defense of their country, their people, and their sanctities, must volunteer to join the army and defense forces to achieve this sacred objective." Source: [https://www.sistani.org/arabic/archive/24918]. This fatwa led to thousands of people to volunteer to support and strengthen the defense forces and the Iraqi army to confront ISIS. Victory was achieved by completely eradicating them and was officially declared on the twenty-sixth of Rabi' al-Awwal in the year 1439 AH. Source: [https://www.sistani.org/Arabic/archive/25876]

even murder. They always bravely stood their ground, never gave up, and protected this legacy so Islam, its immense heritage, the valuable traditions that have been passed down, and its true teachings remain preserved. Looking back at the history of the religious authority, we see that it contributed and sacrificed [immeasurably], and suffered deprivation and scarcity in resources and support, and faced various policies of marginalization, exclusion, and oppression. Yet, after all these years, we still see this entity working at its best, serving its cause in the loftiest of manners. This proves to us that it must be under God's watch, and under Imam Mahdi's care and prayers. Otherwise such an entity would not be able to continue under these conditions.

5. Preserving the independence of the economic decisions made by the seminary

The jurists place a high importance on the seminary's economic independence, no matter the resulting financial hardship, scarcity, and difficult circumstances. These trustworthy jurists abstain from accepting any gifts from governments, civil authorities, or foreign entities. They rely entirely on the religious dues given to them by the believers who seek to discharge their religious obligations by paying zakat, khums, and other types of religious dues. Thus, the seminary remains free from any outside influence and pressure.

The Religious Authority's Approach to Dealing with Public Affairs

Based on the aforementioned significance of the religious authority, its role, and its priorities, it is clear that it operates with a specific approach in dealing with public affairs in order to preserve fairness, wisdom, and rationality in all its decisions. The features of this approach are as follows:

1) The religious authority adheres to a rational method in examining the de facto circumstances, diagnosing the issue at hand, formulating a solution, and finally, implementing a plan and taking a certain position.[17]
2) Peaceful coexistence of people from different sects of Islam, such as Sunnis and Shia, and with people of different religions.[18]
3) Respect for the country's agencies and institutions that have been formed by the people. This applies to the military, security apparatus, political entities, and social and administrative branches.[19] This

---

17. 13 Shawwal 1425 AH, from a confirmed and documented discourse by His Eminence to some scholars during a visit.

18. 12 Muharram 1441 AH (September 12, 2019) https://www.sistani.org/files-new/Archeives/1441h/12-9-2019.pdf

19. 12 Muharram 1441 AH (September 12, 2019) https://www.sistani.org/files-new/Archeives/1441h/12-9-2019.pdf

includes prohibiting the usurpation of property and violation of the law of the land.[20]

4) The view that the Shia must integrate in the land in which they live. This means they allow the lawmakers of their country to appropriately manage their affairs without interfering except if asked to do so or if they deem it necessary based on their circumstances.[21] In fact, in some non-Muslim countries, and for the sake of the greater Muslim good, Muslims may be required to take political positions, affiliate with parties, and join ministries and parliaments. Such decisions must [only] be taken after experts have analyzed the situation of the Muslims therein and confirmed the need for Muslim involvement for some benefit.[22]

5) To not get involved in the details of politics and leave its administration to political specialists and experts. Rather, the only pretext for getting involved in crucial matters that concern the nation as a whole is the inability of the political powers to solve the problems or provide solutions for them.[23]

---

20. 27 Ramadan 1418 AH, from the Sayyid's book *Al-fiqh li al-mughtaribin* (A Code of Practice for Muslims in the West), p.167 and onward .https://www.sistani.org/arabic/book/17/960

21. 12 Muharram 1441 AH (September 12, 2019) https://www.sistani.org/files-new/Archeives/1441h/12-9-2019.pdf

22. 27 Ramadan 1418, from the Sayyid's book *Al-fiqh li al-mughtaribin* (A Code of Practice for Muslims in the West), p.171. https://www.sistani.org/arabic/book/17/960

23. 12 Muharram 1441 AH (September 12, 2019) https://www.sistani.org/files-new/Archeives/1441h/12-9-2019.pdf

Responsibility of the believers towards the jurists, the seminary, and the religious authority during the time of occultation.

The believers have a number of responsibilities and duties they must fulfill in order to achieve the lofty goals that foster their honor and status by protecting the religion God has sent through his prophets and messengers to keep them on the straight path. This complements the sacrifices of the jurists and their vigilance over the interests of Islam and Muslims. Hence, the religious authority recommends a number of things, including:

1) Opponents have realized the importance, position, and role that the religious authority plays, particularly the religious authority in Najaf. Moreover, they know that the religious authorities in the holy cities of Qom and Najaf have maintained a harmonious relationship, which is something they do not want.[24] They also know the religious authority's role in clarifying the purpose and application of Islamic laws, educating people, and guiding them to the righteous path of religion. As such, the purpose behind such various campaigns, which are continuous and unabating, and are intensively trying to smear and taint Shiism, becomes evident. The aim is to overthrow or disable the religious authority and sever the people

---

24. 13 Shawwal 1435 AH, from a confirmed and documented discourse by His Eminence to some scholars during a visit

from the scholars, thus making it easier to defeat Shiism.[25]

2) One of the most important ways that the opponents of Shiism are trying to achieve this goal is by targeting the seminary of the holy city of Najaf and tainting its significance in the Shia community and the Islamic world. The seminary of the holy city of Najaf has a special status because it has been the stronghold and the source of religious knowledge and heritage for more than a thousand years. There is not a single religious scholar who is not indebted, either directly or indirectly, to the seminary of Najaf. Therefore, it is constantly targeted by enemies because they know that destroying it means eradicating the past, the present, and the future of Shiism.[26]

3) The necessity of staying vigilant and cautious to the propaganda, rumors, and allegations that are spread and circulated by enemies. These are usually presented in various subtle, yet appealing ways, and must be recognized so one does not fall in the trap of believing in and spreading them. It is necessary to be aware, pay attention, and refer to the pious scholars to verify and be certain of everything that is said about them and this ancient seminary in order to uncover the true facts and not get involved in matters that diminish its rights and its reputation.[27]

---

25. Sunday, 22 Jumada al-Ula 1435 AH, from a confirmed and documented discourse by His Eminence to some scholars during a visit.

26. Ibid.

27. Ibid

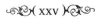

4) The believers must always defend the religious authority, and not just because a particular scholar should be defended, but rather because of the importance of the religious authority as an immutable and public institution.[28] Defending the religious authority means defending the religion and the sect, because the source of its strength is a group of current and active religious authority that is intimately familiar with the era and culture it is in, and knows how to navigate and guide the people as needed. [29]

---

28. Ibid

29. 13 Shawwal 1435 AH, from a confirmed and documented discourse by His Eminence to some scholars during a visit.

Part One

···············◆·◆·◆···············

General Advice, Tips, and Instructions

The honorable reader will find here a set of advice, recommendations, and guidelines directed to the believers in general, followed by a special section for women, a section for the youth, and a section on awaiting the Imam of our time. The final four chapters cover matters related to the public, society, and political affairs.

General advice, tips, and instructions

Pearl 1: The importance of seeking knowledge

Seeking knowledge is a necessity. Knowledge is one of the components that strengthen a nation because it is the basis for the development of the individual as well as society and its institutions. One should focus on and give importance to specializing in fields that serve the people.[30] Furthermore, one should become familiar with three books which will foster contemplation and reflection:

1. The first and most preeminent is the Holy Quran because it is the seal of God's message to His creation. It was sent to revive the deep intellects, ignite the springs of wisdom, and soften the hardness of the hearts. It reveals the circumstances [of life, which one must learn] by posing examples. One must not neglect reciting this book while cultivating the feeling that they are listening to

---

30. 13 Shawwal 1435 AH, from a talk the Sayyid gave to some of his visitor students and scholars. It has been confirmed documented.

God's conversation with them. He, the Most High, revealed His Book as a message to His creation.

2. The second book is Nahj al-Balaghah,[31] which in general explains the contents and references of the Holy Quran in an eloquent manner that stimulates a spirit of contemplation, reflection, education, and wisdom. One should not abandon reading this book whenever they have an opportunity or some free time. They should imagine they are in the audience of one of Imam Ali's sermons.[32] In addition,

---

31. This book is a number of selected sermons, letters, and quotes by Imam Ali (p). They have been gathered together in one book by the jurist, Sayyid Muhammad bin al-Hussain, known as al-Sharif al-Radi. (406 AH).

32. His Eminence has a detailed comment about Nahj al-balagha in which he states, "This honorable book contains the words of our master, the Commander of the Faithful, which are considered the most eloquent of speech. These occur after the words of God Almighty and the words of his chosen Prophet (pbuh&hp). This is because this book shows the natural and intellectual way of thinking and reflecting upon this universe, it explains the Islamic beliefs and their characteristics, it clarifies the laws and practical aspects of this life that should be implemented in order to tame the soul and perfect it, it explains the Sharia laws and the obligations that branch from it, it reminds us of the etiquette required to follow God's laws, and it teaches us how to praise God and supplicate to Him, and many more lessons. On the other hand, it also mirrors Islamic history and the events that occurred after the Prophet, and specifically during the time of the caliphate of the Imam. It includes important aspects of the Imam's biography, morals, attributes, knowledge and jurisprudence. The Muslims in general should seek enlightenment in the matters of their religion by learning and reading this book. They should be interested to study it, reflect upon it, and memorize parts of it, especially the young among them. It is also appropriate for those who claim to love the Imam and wish that they were in his time, to do so by reading his sermons and be guided by them and follow his path through this book. The Imam said in the Battle of the

one should also pay close attention to Imam Ali's will (letter) that he left for his son al-Hasan because it was written by him for this very purpose.[33]

3. The third book is Sahifa al-Sajjadiya,[34] which contains eloquent supplications that derive their contents from the Holy Quran and teachings of what a person should strive for of interests, concerns, vision, and ambition. It also describes accountability of the self and how a person should critique and reflect upon the secrets of their soul, especially the supplication of Makarim al-Akhlaq, the Honorable Virtues.[35]

Pearl 2: Having a spirit of learning and cultivating wisdom

A person must possess the spirit of learning and a desire to increase their wisdom and knowledge in all

---

Camel that some people who were at the war with him "were not born yet", and by that he meant those who came later. Because God knew they had a sincere intention and wished to be with the Imam and follow his footsteps, they will be resurrected with the Imam on the day of judgment, and moreover, it is because they walked in the footsteps of the Imam without being apologetic about it and without following heresies and suspicions.

33. 28 Safar 1437 AH, Advice to Youth, https://www.sistani.org/arabic/archive/25237

34. This book is a collection of unique and rare supplications and prayers that have been narrated on by Imam Ali Bin Al-Hussein (p), known as Zain Al-Abidin. It has been printed and published under the name al-Sahifah al-sajjadiyyah, and it is a widely known and circulated copy.

35. 28 Rabi al-Awwal 1437 AH, from his advice for the youth. Source: [https://www.sistani.org/arabic/archive/25237]

stages of their life. They should deeply contemplate their actions and attributes and their respective consequences on themselves and on their surroundings, and the events and outcomes that take place around them. By learning from life's everyday lessons, one increases their knowledge, experience, and virtue. This life is a school of multiple dimensions and depths. Everything that happens therein has either a lesson or a sign, and in every incident, there is a message and meaning, which only reveal themselves to those who contemplate and seek morals and lessons from them. So, one should not neglect learning from this life and deriving the knowledge and experience it has to offer until they return to God. The more insight a person acquires, the richer they will be in wisdom and the more they will recognize [the fruits of] experience and potential errors. God Almighty has said in the Holy Quran, God gives wisdom to anyone whom He wants. Whoever is given wisdom, certainly, has received much good. Only people of reason can grasp this."[36] God Almighty even tells his Prophet to ask for more knowledge, Say, My Lord, Grant me more knowledge,"[37] [38]

Pearl 3: Paying attention to prayer

Do not slacken in giving importance to your obligatory prayers. The best deed a person comes to God Almighty with is their prayer. Prayer teaches the person how to behave in God's presence and it is the salutation that

---

36. The Holy Quran, 2:269.

37. The Holy Quran, 20:114.

38. 28 Rabi al-Awwal 1437 AH, from his advice for the youth. Source: [https://www.sistani.org/arabic/archive/25237]

they present to Him. It is what preserves religion and it is the basis for the acceptance of all other deeds. God Almighty has made it convenient to perform based on the circumstances and in the event of apprehension. God Almighty has said in the Holy Quran, "Pay due attention to your prayers, especially the middle prayer and stand up while praying, in obedience to God."[39] [40]

Pearl 4: Acquiring the manners and ethics of the Prophet and his progeny

Ensure that you embody the manners and ethics of the Prophet and his family when you deal with others so you are an ornament for Islam and an example of its values. This religion is formulated according to human nature, sound intellect, and perfect ethics, and suffice it to say, it raised the banner of reasoning and morality as its universal message. At its core, it calls its followers to ponder and think carefully before acting and deciding what to do in all aspects of this life. Similarly, its legislative system is based on stimulating the untapped regions of our minds and instinct [to better understand our purpose as creation]. God Almighty says in the Holy Quran, "And by the soul and that (Power) which designed it, and inspired it with knowledge of evil and piety, those who purify their souls will certainly have everlasting happiness, and those who corrupt their souls will certainly be deprived (of happiness)."[41] In addition, it has

---

39. The Holy Quran, 2:238

40. 22 Rabial-Akhir,1436. Advice and recommendations given by the Sayyid. [https://www.sistani.org/arabic/archive/25034]

41. The Holy Quran, 91:7.

been narrated that Imam Ali (p) said, "He has sent His messengers and prophets, one after the other, to the people to lead them to their own binding nature and remind them of the blessings they've forgotten, and use their preaching [to them] as proof of God, and entice what they have buried in their minds."[42] If Muslims develop a deeper understanding [of their religion] and follow the teachings of religion carefully, they will see immense blessings that will light up their lives.[43]

All of our Imams have commanded us to mind our manners and ethics, even with those who oppose us in our thinking. Shias should deal with all people, even those who are against them and oppose their ideology, with the best manners possible, even if the other side is being offensive. This is what is related in many traditions, which point to the demeanor of the infallibles and how they instructed their followers and dealt with those who opposed them. It has been narrated by Muawiyah bin Wahab: "I asked Imam al-Sadiq, 'How do we deal with those who are from our own people but don't ascribe to our way?' He replied, 'Look at the [example of the] Imams who you emulate and do as they do. By God, they visit their sick acquaintances, attend their funerals, bear witness by and for them, and return what they were entrusted with to them.'"[44] The manners and ethics that the Imams enjoined us to practice, even with those who oppose us, clearly proves the basis for our values and

---

42. Al Sharif al Radi, *Nahj al balagha*, Sermon 1.

43. 22 Rabi al Awwal 1436 AH, General advice. Source: [https://sistani.org/arabic/archive/25034]

44. Al Kafi, Shaykh al Kulayni, Vol. 2, p. 365.

gives people a practical and true representation of the true path of Ahl al-Bayt.

Similarly, it has been narrated from Mudrik bin Zuhair that he said, "Abu Abdullah Jafar bin Muhammed said, 'Convey salutations, mercy and blessings upon our companions, and tell them God is merciful upon those who foster love for us in the hearts of others by telling them about the goodness [of our way] and denial [of what we considered to be evil].'"[45]

It has also been narrated by Abi Osama Zaid al-Shaham that he said, "Abu Abuallah said to me, 'Convey my salutations to those who you find obeying me and accepting what I preach. And, I remind you to be pious and vigilant in [adherence to] your religion, to expend effort for the sake of God, to speak the truth, to return/fulfill what has been entrusted to you, to lengthen your prostration, and to be good to your neighbors, for that is what Muhammed called people towards. Fulfill what has been entrusted to you, whether by someone who is righteous or a sinner because the Messenger of God used to command people to do so for the suture and that which is sutured. Reach out to your kin, attend their funerals, visit their sick and give them their rights. If any of you is vigilant in their religion, tells the truth, gives back/fulfills the trust, and has a good nature with people, then they will say this person is a Jafari and that will make me happy because they will say these are the characteristics of Jafar. On the other hand, if any of you is the opposite of that, I will feel offended because people will say these

---

45. Al-Saduq, al-amali, p.159.

are the bad manners of Jafar. I swear by God, my father told me, 'if a person amongst the people was from the Shia of Ali he would be the most trustworthy, the fairest in giving others their rights, the most truthful, and people would entrust him with their directives and valuable possessions. If that tribe was asked about them, it would say, 'there is no one like so-and-so, they are the most honest and most truthful amongst us.'"[46] Another narration by ibn Abi Yaafur states, "Abu Abdullah said, 'Invite others [to our path] without having to use your tongues (i.e., words), so that [instead] they may observe in you piety, effort, prayer, and goodness, for these actions are the best invitation [to our faith].'"[47] An authentic narration by Abu Osama (Zaid l-Shaham) who said, "I heard Abu Abdullah say, 'Always remember to be pious, God-fearing, diligent, truthful, trustworthy, good natured, and good to your neighbors. Call others towards you without using your tongues (i.e., through your actions and not your words). Be an ornament and do not be a source of shame [for us]. Prolong your bowing and prostration because when one of you does so, Iblis will stand behind them and yell, 'Woe upon him/her! They obeyed God while I disobeyed, and they prostrated to God while I refused.'"[48] [49]

---

46. Al-kulayni, *al-kafi*, vol.2, p.636.

47. Al-kulayni, *al-kafi*, vol.2, p.78.

48. Al-Majlisi, vol.67, p.299.

49. 13 Shawwal 1435 AH, from a confirmed and documented discourse by His Eminence to some scholars during a visit.

Pearl 5: Mastering your crafts and specialties

One should give importance and special attention to their vocation and specialty until they become proficient in it. They should not speak without knowledge nor should they act without experience. They should excuse themselves from anything they are not capable of doing or anything they do not know, or seek help from others who are more experienced because it is better for them that they are trustworthy. People should also perform their jobs with passion, motivation, and enthusiasm, and they should not be solely concerned with earning money, especially from a prohibited source, because there is no blessing in money acquired from a prohibited source. Furthermore, whoever collects money from an illegitimate source is not safe from God opening a door of calamity upon them, and then they will be forced to spend what they collected to alleviate the suffering and hardship they brought upon themselves. Forbidden money will not enrich you in the life of this world and it will be a heavy burden in the afterlife.

Among the various professions, let **doctors** especially heed this [aforementioned] advice because they are dealing with human lives and bodies. Thus, they should be very careful not to make a mistake that resulted from speaking without knowledge or acting without experience because it will very quickly end in horrendous consequences. Indeed, God Almighty has said, "Woe to those who are fraudulent in (weighing and measuring), those who demand a full measure from others, but when they measure or weigh, give less.

Do they not realize that they will be resurrected?"[50] Also, the Prophet once said, "God Almighty loves if one of you does a job that they master it."[51]

College students and professors should also familiarize themselves with all the different aspects of their profession and make sure they are up-to-date on all the new developments that are emerging in the centers of knowledge. This is especially important in medicine where it is critical that knowledge and practice are modern and in conformity with what is new in the field. They should always research advances in science by consulting beneficial articles and reviewing novel discoveries so that they can compete with other leading centers of science and research with the resources available to them. They should strive to be more than mere students of others and consumers of equipment and tools that others create. Instead, they should strive to innovate and contribute to expanding and invigorating the knowledge base, just like their forefathers spearheaded and pioneered the sciences in past centuries. Yet, no nation is more worthy than another in achieving this. Thus, support and nurture the intelligent youth, especially those with high aptitude, even if they come from humble backgrounds. Help them, just like you would your own children, acquire the highest degree of beneficial knowledge, so

---

50. The Holy Quran, 83: 1-4.

51. 28 Rabi al-Awwal 1437 AH, from his advice for the youth. Source: [https://www.sistani.org/arabic/archive/25237]

that you may gain from what they achieve and your society and next generations prosper as a result.[52]

Pearl 6: Use your own expectations as a guide for how you treat others

Every person should consider their own expectations as a basis for how they interact with others. Thus, one should treat others the way they would like to be treated, and should be good to others, just as they hope for God to be good to them. The ethics of any endeavor should always be observed so that one does not engage in ways that are ultimately demeaning and cause embarrassment. Every worker and professional should know that they have been entrusted by their superior for the work they are doing, and so, must work based on that trust and deliver excellent work. They must also not betray any trust or breach any contract, and they should be particularly cautious about doing so unknowingly because God is watching and monitoring their deeds, and they will be asked about it sooner or later. Treachery and betrayal are of the ugliest acts in the eyes of God, and they result in the most dangerous consequences.[53]

Pearl 7: Promoting love and affection

The spirit of love and affection should prevail amongst the believers. This is because a believer has rights, and

---

52. 28 Rabi al-Awwal 1437 AH, from his advice for the youth. Source: [https://www.sistani.org/arabic/archive/25237]

53. 28 Rabi al-Awwal 1437 AH, from his advice for the youth. Source: [https://www.sistani.org/arabic/archive/25237]

as such, it has been narrated that, "A true believer loves for their brother/sister what they love for themselves."[54] This means that a person should be genuinely happy for any good that their fellow believer has achieved, as if they had achieved it themselves. If their fellow believer was granted money, they should be pleased for them as if they were the ones to have acquired it. Similarly, they should be pleased for the achievement of a fellow believer's child as if it were their own child.[55]

Pearl 8: Promoting a spirit of cooperation, solidarity, and compassion

It is crucial that a spirit of cooperation, solidarity, compassion, and communication, in addition to love, be fostered and maintained amongst the believers. It has been narrated by Abdallah ibn Bukair from another man, who said, "Once a group of us entered upon Abu Jafar and said, 'O' son of the Messenger of God, we want to travel to Iraq, so what do you advise us?' Abu Jaafar responded, 'Let your strong strengthen your weak and let your rich aid your poor...'"[56] It has also been reported that Abu Jafar Muhammed Ibn Ali advised one of his companions to pass this advice to his followers: "Send our regards to our Shia and advise them to be God-fearing and pious, and that their rich should aid their poor, their healthy should visit their sick, their

---

54. Bihar al-Anwar, al-Majlisi, vol.71, p.222.

55. 13 Shawwal 1435 AH, from a confirmed and documented discourse by His Eminence to some scholars during a visit.

56. Al-kulayni, al-Kafi, vol.2, p.222.

living should honor the funerals of their dead, and they should visit each other's homes because their gatherings enliven our legacy. May God have mercy on those who enliven our legacy and act upon it in the best way. Tell them they will not benefit from us except by doing good deeds, and they will not acquire our guardianship (*wilayah*) except through fear of God. The most regretful people on the Day of Judgment are those who do not practice what they preach."[57] [58]

Pearl 9: Observing and respecting that which is sacred

Be aware of what is sacred to God and do not violate it by your tongue or hands. Also, be careful not to accuse a person for another's sins because God Almighty says, "No one will bear the burden of another."[59] Do not treat an assumption as if it is a firm conclusion because the latter will protect you in such matters while the former is an [unfair] assault on another without valid proof. Moreover, do not let your hatred towards your enemy lead you to violating their rights, as God Almighty has said, "Believers, be steadfast for the cause of God and just in bearing witness. Let not a group's hostility to you cause you to deviate from justice. Be

57. Mirza al-Nuri, *Mustadrak al-wasail,* vol.8, p.311.

58. 13 Shawwal 1435 AH, from a confirmed and documented discourse by His Eminence to some scholars during a visit.

59. The Holy Quran, 35:18.

just, for it is closer to piety. Have fear of God; God is Well Aware of what you do."[60] [61]

Pearl 10: Observing the rights of other people and their wealth

Be extremely careful when dealing with other people's money. Another Muslim's money is not permissible for you [to take] unless they give it to you by their own free and good will. Whoever has forcefully usurped the property of another has earned flames for themselves from the fire of hell. God Almighty has said, "Those who wrongfully consume the property of orphans are, in fact, consuming fire in their bellies, and they will suffer the blazing fire."[62] [63]

Pearl 11: The danger and reprehensibility of prejudice

Prejudice, which is reprehensible, should always be denounced while adhering to the highest morals and ethics. This is because God has made people into nations and tribes so they may get to know one another and exchange beneficial things to help each other. Do not allow narrowmindedness and personal prejudices to overcome. It is quite evident that many believers,

---

60. The Holy Quran, 5:8.

61. 22 Rabi al-Awwal 1436 AH, General advice. Source: [https://www.sistani.org/arabic/archive/25034]

62. The Holy Quran, 4:10.

63. 22 Rabi al-Awwal 1436 AH, General advice. Source: [https://www.sistani.org/arabic/archive/25034]

and Muslims in general, in many countries are wasting their energies, strength, and wealth to defeat one another rather than investing them in developing the sciences, cultivating [mutually beneficial] resources, and improving people's conditions. "Guard yourselves against discord among yourselves so that it will not mislead anyone of you, especially the unjust, and know that God's retribution is most severe,"[64] thus, if discord befalls you, then try to extinguish it and prevent it from spreading, and "All of you united hold fast to the rope of God (the Quran and His Messenger)."[65] Know that if God sees goodness in your heart, He will bless you with better than what He has taken from you. After all, He is capable of everything.[66]

Pearl 12: Good guardianship

It is very important for anyone who has been given guardianship over something to execute it properly, whether it concerns their family or the society in which they live. As such, fathers should take good care of their children, spouses should take care of each other and their families and never resort to violence and cruelty even if the circumstance requires firmness. Instead, they should resort to wisdom in order to keep their family and society healthy. Means of [dealing with others with] firmness are not limited to physical abuse or profanity, rather, there are other practical approaches and methods, like consulting people with

64. The Holy Quran,

65. The Holy Quran, 3:103.

66. 22 Rabi al-Akhir, 1436. Advice and recommendations given by the Sayyid. [https://www.sistani.org/arabic/archive/25034]

experience, that a wise person can find. Moreover, harsh ways often have the opposite effect of what is desired, they worsen the problem and make it more rooted in the person one is trying to correct. There is no good in firmness that requires an unjust intervention nor in remedying a mistake with a sin.

Similarly, any person who is given a societal responsibility must carry it out in the best way possible, acting as an advisor to the members of society and not betraying them if they neglect fulfilling their duties. Verily, God is the guardian over all their affairs, and He will severely question all of them on the Day of Judgement. Thus, the person should not spend people's money inappropriately and should not make decisions other than what will benefit them. Nor should they use their position [of authority] to form a [private] group of accomplices who cover up for each other and exchange prohibited wealth and benefits, and prevent others from positions they rightfully deserve or services they require. The person's work should be equally beneficial for everyone without any favoritism towards certain individuals due to family or friendly relationships. Focusing solely on personal acquaintances rather than fulfilling the rights of the general public is unfairness and corruption. If anyone should be favored, it is those in need who are helpless and do not have any recourse or help except God.

The person assigned guardianship must not use religion or sectarianism as a basis for who benefits from their work and services. Rather, their work should be based on the true values that all religions are based on, such as truth, justice, honesty, and other core moral values.

God Almighty says in the Holy Quran, "We sent Our Messengers with clear evidence (to support their truthfulness), and sent with them the Book and the Balance so that people would maintain justice. We sent down iron - in which there is strong power and benefit for the people - so that God would know who would help Him and His Messenger without seeing the unseen. God is All-powerful and Majestic."[67] Also, Amir al-Muminin said in his letter to Malik al-Ashtar, "I heard the Prophet say in more than one place, 'A community that does not secure the rights of the weak from the strong is not safe from disturbance.'"[68] Hence, whoever acts according to other than these values, they will have decorated themselves with false hopes and wealth. Verily, Prophet Muhammad (pbuh&hp), Imam Ali (p), and the martyr Hussain were the most deserving of leading the people because of their unfettered justice, and because their actions matched their words and followed their [declared] way. Whoever is appointed in a position of guardianship should read the letter that Imam Ali sent to Malik al-Ashtar when he appointed him as the governor of Egypt because it describes the principles of justice and how to fulfill a trust. Furthermore, it is not only beneficial for those who are guardians, but also to anyone who bears any responsibility, and the more responsibility that falls on the person, the more necessary it is to implement these values.[69]

---

67. The Holy Quran, 57:25.

68. Bihar al-anwar, Al-majlisi, vol.74, p.258.

69. 28 Rabi al-Awwal 1437 AH, from his advice for the youth. Source: [https://www.sistani.org/arabic/archive/25237]

Pearl 13: Muslim Unity

It is highly necessary that Muslims focus on unity and implementation and establishment of love and affection between the members of this *ummah*. The bare minimum is a peaceful coexistence based on mutual respect and free from any conflict or sectarian/denominational attack, irrespective of its cause. After all, everyone believes in the One God, the Prophet's message, the return [to God], the position of the Holy Quran and the sunnah of the Prophet as the source of religious laws, and love for the family of the prophet. This is all in addition to the acts that all Muslims practice and which are a foundation of Islam such as prayer, fasting, pilgrimage (haj), and other shared principles that are the basis of a united Muslim nation.[70]

Pearl 14: A choice between hatred and aggression or love and dialogue

I repeat my call to our zealous sons and daughters of different sects and ethnicities to be aware of the danger that threatens their future, and to stand together and condemn hatred and violence and replace it with love and peaceful dialogue to resolve their conflicts. It is necessary to resort to dialogue to solve conflicts rather than violence and killing. I remind those who shed Muslim blood and indiscriminately kill innocent souls of what the Prophet said in his farewell pilgrimage, "your blood, your money, and your honor are just as sacred as the day in this month and in this nation. Whoever

---

70. 14 Muharram 1428 AH. Source:
[https://www.sistani.org/arabic/statement/1504]

hears this from me now should relay it to whoever did not hear it from me." The Prophet (pbuh&hp) has also said, "Whoever witnesses that there is no God but Allah and that Muhammad is the messenger of God, then their blood and money become are protected from any harm."[71] He also said, "Whoever aids in the killing of a fellow Muslim, even by half a word, will meet God on judgment day labeled with 'Desperate for God's mercy' between his eyes."[72] [73]

Pearl 15: Human fellowship and social engagement

We are all brothers and sisters in humanity and belong to one nation. I specifically address those who harm non-Muslim citizens, such as Christians, Sabians and others. Have you not heard what Imam Ali (p) said when he was told a non-Muslim woman was being harassed by so-called Muslims and they were trying to steal her jewelry? He said, "If some [true] Muslim [heard about this incident and] died in a state of regret and remorse [due to this injustice], then I would not blame them, rather I would consider them worthy [of being called a Muslim]."[74] Thus, why do you harm your brothers and sisters in humanity and your fellow citizens? The sanctity of life and the role of others in solving problems, which should replace aggression with

71. Bihar al-Anwar, *Al-majlisi*, vol.23, p.96.

72. Al-kafi, *al-Kulayni*, vol.2, p.368.

73. 22 Jumada al-Akhira AH 1427. Source: [https://www.sistani.org/arabic/statement/1499]

74. George Jordac, Masterpieces of Nahj al-balagha, p.30

just dialogue and equity, should be respected on the basis of observing the rights and responsibilities of all citizens while avoiding sectarian or ethnic conflicts.[75]

Pearl 16: Prohibition of offending non-Muslims

Beware of offending non-Muslims or violating their rights, regardless of their religion or sect, because they are living under the protection of Muslims. Therefore, anyone who violates their rights is treacherous [to Islam's way], and treachery is one of the worse violations against human nature and God's religion. God commanded us in the Holy Quran saying, "God does not forbid you to deal kindly and justly with those who have not fought against you about the religion or expelled you from your homes. God does not love the unjust people."[76] A Muslim should not accept or permit that the rights of a non-Muslim who is living in the protection and care of Muslims are violated.[77] The same applies if a Muslim lives in a non-Islamic country, they should also respect and not harm those around them.[78] Rather, a Muslim

---

75. 22 Jumada al-Akhira AH 1427. Source: [https://www.sistani.org/arabic/statement/1499]

76. The Holy Quran, 60:8.

77. 22 Rabi al-Akhir, 1436. Advice and recommendations given by the Sayyid. [https://www.sistani.org/arabic/archive/25034] Also: Al-Sistani, *Al-fiqh li al-mughtaribin* (A Code of Practice for Muslims in the West), the chapter on dealing with laws,p.167. Source: https://www.sistani.org/arabic/book/17/960.

78. Al-Sistani, *Al-fiqh li al-mughtaribin* (A Code of Practice for Muslims in the West), p.168, q.219. Source: [https://www.sistani.org/arabic/book/17/960].

should live among their fellow community members, interact [cordially] with them, befriend and treat them well, be a good neighbor, and join in their happiness and congratulate them on their holidays and important occasions.[79]

Pearl 17: The importance of respecting others and their beliefs

It is obligatory to respect other people and their beliefs. Freedom of speech and expression of one's opinion does not justify attacking the beliefs of others and what they consider to be sacred because this creates an environment of tension, conflict, and aggression.

Pearl 18: Self-discipline

The religious authority emphasizes the importance of having the highest levels of self-discipline and control. People should be vigilant that their actions do not offend others, and remember the words of God: "Believers, be steadfast for the cause of God and just in bearing witness. Let not a group's hostility to you cause you to deviate from justice. Be just, for it is closer to piety. Have fear of God; God is Well Aware of what you

79. Al-Sistani, *Al-fiqh li al-mughtaribin* (A Code of Practice for Muslims in the West), p.168, q.308 & q.309. Source: [https://www.sistani.org/arabic/book/17/960].

do."[80] [81] As such, Muslims should abide by the laws of the country they are living in.[82]

Guidelines for Believers Regarding Their Duty Towards Imam al-Mahdi (may God hasten his return)

Pearl 19: Adherence to Islamic laws (Sharia)

There is no doubt that the best means of obeying the Imam, getting close to him, and gaining his satisfaction is by adhering to the sacred laws of Islam, acquiring virtues, staying away from vices, and following the path of the esteemed scholars, leaders of the sect, and the people of insight, who have continued [this effort] since the era of the Imams. Thus, anyone who follows a deviated or innovated path has plunged into murkiness and strife, and has strayed from their [true] purpose.[83]

Pearl 20: Seeking recourse in the religious authority in the time of occultation

The [only] recourse for believers in matters of religion during the time of occultation are the pious scholars. Hence, if a person confirms their Islamic knowledge

---

80. The Holy Quran, 5:8.

81. 29 Ramadan 1431 AH. Source: [https://www.sistani.org/arabic/statement/1513].

82. 9 Dhu al-Hijjah 1441 AH. Source: [https://www.sistani.org/arabic/archive/26453]

83. 12 Safar 1428 AH, fatwa. Source: [https://www.sistani.org/arabic/archive/25699].

and the validity of their actions, and knows that they avoid temptation and deviation, then they must follow them because this is the approach of this sect since the beginning of the minor occultation to our era.[84]

Pearl 21: Connecting to the Imam during his occultation

Among the most important duties of the believers during the time of the Imam's occultation is to be very cautious and careful with regards to everything related to him, his reappearance, and the ways to connect with him. This is one of the hardest challenges and source of trials in the entire era of occultation.[85]

Pearl 22: Claims of meeting the Imam

Our religious stance towards those who claim that they have met the Imam during the time of occultation, either directly or through a vision (dream), is to deny what they say and reject their claims and anything they attribute to him. Rather, whatever they attribute to the Imam, such as [his putative] words, which are known to be false, should be denied.[86]

---

84. 12 Safar 1428 AH, fatwa. Source: [https://www.sistani.org/arabic/archive/25699].

85. 12 Safar 1428 AH, fatwa. Source: [https://www.sistani.org/arabic/archive/25699].

86. 21 Ramadan 1424 AH, fatwa. Source: [/http://www.aqaed.com/faq/3049].

Pearl 23: The stance towards false claims

We call upon the believers (may God enable them to achieve what pleases Him) to avoid being drawn into false claims about the Imam and not contribute to the dissemination or promotion of this disinformation in any way. They should be wary of people behind these claims and their followers as long as they persist with this falseness.[87]

Pearl 24: How to understand and apply narrations about Imam Mahdi (may God hasten his return)

The narrations that describe the signs of reappearance are just like other traditions narrated from the Ahl al-Bayt in that they should be verified as credible by referring back to the experts in this matter who can examine them and distinguish the weak ones from the strong and the apparent from the implied, and who can weigh between their contradictions. Thus, it is incorrect to try to understand the meaning behind these narrations by using personal references, guessing, or making assumptions. As such, assumptions do not aid in a person's understanding of the truth.[88]

---

87. 21 Ramadan 1424 AH, fatwa. Source:
[/http://www.aqaed.com/faq/3049].

88. 12 Safar 1428 AH. Source:
[https://www.sistani.org/arabic/archive/25699].

Guidelines for social and political matters including elections and politicians

Many prestigious dignitaries from around the world come to visit the religious authority and listen and benefit for its spiritual, social, and moral advice and recommendations.[89] In addition, many social and political figures from the global community of believers seek an audience with the religious authority and request answers to their religious questions and clarifications on their social and political issues to help them make

89. Various important visits have happened in the past. Many dignitaries, such as kings, presidents, and officials of prestigious international organizations have visited the current religious authority His Eminence Sayyid Ali al-Sistani in his office. One of the most important was the visit of the Secretary-General of the United Nations, Mr. Ban Ki-moon to Najaf on 24 July 2014. Mr. Ban Ki-moon announced his visit through the media and an official statement on the United Nations' website. The statement read, "...I strongly welcome his crucially important appeal for all citizens to exercise the highest degree of restraint, to work on strengthening the bonds between each other and avoid any kind of behavior that may affect the unity of Iraq. To demonstrate to him the United Nations' approval of his efforts, which aim to protect civilians in the current conflicts, I expressed to His Eminence how deeply moved I was by his consistent calls for all sides to refrain from sectarian or ethnic rhetoric." Mr. Ban Ki-moon also said, "He is a man of the deepest wisdom and tolerance. He is an inspiration and a role model for his many followers in Iraq and beyond. I am extremely honored to have met His Eminence Grand Ayatollah al-Sistani today for the first time. Once again, I was deeply impressed by my time with His Eminence. You can continue to count on my full support along with the United Nations as the people of Najaf and all of Iraq work to build a tolerant, peaceful and prosperous country for all its people."
[http://www.un.org/sg/offthecuff/index.asp?nid=3496].

better decisions that adhere to the sharia and fulfill their obligations. Due to the importance of these recommendations and advice, it is important to mention some of them here for everyone's benefit.

Pearl 25: Guidelines for governors and politicians

Muslim men in a position of leadership should strongly consider the guidelines expressed by Imam Ali (p) about their roles in Nahjul Balagha so that they can use his approach and method in the fulfillment of their obligation. Moreover, they should think of themselves as his followers, and in showing their desire to follow in his footsteps, implement his words and efforts into their own government and society.[90][91]

---

90. This book is a number of selected sermons, letters, and quotes by Imam Ali (p). They have been gathered together in one book by the jurist, Sayyid Muhammad bin al-Hussain, known as al-Sharif al-Radi. (406 AH).

We emphasize the importance of the letter that Imam Ali (p) sent to Malik al-Ashtar when he assigned him as the governor of Egypt. It is letter 53 in the volume of letters of Nahj al-Balagha. It is worth mentioning that the United Nations, through the Secretary-general, has spoken of the importance of this letter in protecting human rights and dignity, and in showing that all humans are equal, a person is either your brother in faith or your brother in humanity.
[https://www.un.org/press/en/1997/19971209.SGSM6419.html].

91. 26 Rajab 1433 AH. from a confirmed and documented discourse by His Eminence to some scholars during a visit .

Pearl 26: The role of the government

The most important role of the government is to establish social justice, maintain security, fight corruption, and preserve national sovereignty.[92]

Pearl 27: The people possess the authority

The religious authority views the **people of a nation as the source of its authority** and no one else. As such, as a nation's constitution stipulates, the government is then assigned its respective authority from the people. The most efficient and safest way to resolve conflicts is by going back to the people[93] and making sure that their will is being respected by using a secret ballot [to determine their opinion on a matter].[94]

Pearl 28: Elections and their requirements

Elections should adhere to certain essential requirements that give their results the highest level of credibility such that the citizens will feel confident to participate. For this reason, they should be conducted under just and fair laws that remain independent of the personal agendas of any political sides or parties. Furthermore,

---

92. 24 Muharram 1442 AH. Source:
[https://www.sistani.org/arabic/archive/26377].

93. 23 Rabi al-Akhir AH. Source:
[https://www.sistani.org/arabic/archive/26370].

94. 17 Rabi al-Awwal AH. Source:
[https://www.sistani.org/arabic/archive/26359].

they should be transparent in all their procedures and tightly supervised.[95]

Pearl 29: Importance of elections and voting

Participating in elections is very important in determining the future of the country and the generations to come, because it decides the laws and supervises all the government entities. Hence, anyone who does not participate in elections is giving their choice to another and relinquishing the opportunity to decide their future and that of their children, which is a major mistake no citizen should make.[96]

Pearl 30: Role of a Muslim in a non-Muslim country

The greater interests of Muslims residing in a non-Muslim country may require them to participate in the government of that country, whether by joining political parties or by taking active roles in governmental agencies and institutions. As such, Muslims should turn to experienced individuals [in the areas of government and politics] to determine the best way and extent they should participate.[97]

---

95. 24 Muharram 1442 AH. Source: [https://www.sistani.org/arabic/archive/26377].

96. 4 Jumada al-Akhira 1435 AH. Friday sermon, and 25 Jumada al-Akhira 1435 AH, Friday sermon.

97. 27 Ramadan 1418 AH. from the Sayyid's book *Al-fiqh li al-mughtaribin* (A Code of Practice for Muslims in the West), the

Pearl 31: Qualities of a candidate

Candidates should be selected according to their qualifications, honesty, diligence, and desire to protect and benefit the country and its citizens.[98]

Pearl 32: Knowing a candidate's history

Citizens should be cautious not to blindly accept false promises and sugar-coated speeches. They should look past a candidate's banners and promotional material that fill the streets and their social media accounts before the elections. Instead, they should research the candidate's history and examine their honesty and suitability [for the position], making sure that they care about the wellbeing of their country and the people before deciding to give them their vote.[99]

Pearl 33: Knowing who to vote for is the citizen's responsibility

The religious authority does not specify which candidate the citizens should vote for. Instead, the religious authority wants the citizens to take full responsibility for researching and voting for the appropriate candidates.[100]

---

chapter on dealing with laws, p.171.
[https://www.sistani.org/arabic/book/17/960].

98. 25 Jumada al-Akhira 1435 AH. Friday sermon.

99. 4 Jumada al-Akhira AH. Friday Sermon.

100. 25 Jumada al-Akhira 1435 AH. Friday sermon.

Pearl 34: Peaceful protest and its conditions

Every citizen has the right to peacefully protest and express their opinion and demand their rights. Each citizen has the freedom to use this right and no one can require anyone to hold the same opinions as theirs. Also, participating or not participating in protests should not be a reason for one citizen to accuse another [of apathy]. Rather, all citizens must understand that others have different opinions, and they should respect their opinions and respect them for their decision to not participate.[101]

Pearl 35: Defeating Terrorism

Cooperative efforts are needed from everyone to defeat terrorism, regardless of religion, sect, viewpoint, and ethnicity. This is required to protect the homeland, all of its people, and its sacred holy sites from terrorists.[102]

Guidelines for the Youth

Pearl 36: Why advise the youth in particular?

I advise the dear youth, whose affairs I care about deeply, just like I care about the affairs of myself and my family, with these pieces of advice so they may find happiness in both this life and the next. They are the essence of God's message to His creation, good counsel from God's wise, righteous, and faithful servants, and the culmination of my experience and knowledge.

---

101. 25 Jumada al-Akhira 1435 AH. Friday sermon.

102. 12 Ramadan 1435 AH. Friday sermon.

These guidelines are the foundation of firmness and its pillars and only a reminder, such that a person finds the light of truth, clarity of human nature (fitra), proof of intellect, and the different experiences of life prescribed by the divine message and the sermons of the insightful. Thus, every person should heed these guidelines and implement them throughout their life, especially the youth, who are in the prime of their physical and mental strength and have the most valuable of a person's possessions at their fingertips. It is important to note that if one cannot achieve and implement all of these guidelines, then they should at least adhere to some of them because small steps are better than no steps at all and achieving something is better than not achieving anything at all. God says, "Whoever has done an atom's weight of good, will see it and whoever has done an atom's weight of evil, will also see it." [103] [104]

Pearl 37: The importance of believing in God and the afterlife

It is crucial for the youth to have a firm conviction in God and the afterlife. Thus, none of you should abandon it under any circumstance, especially given the clear evidence and righteous approach that points to its verity. Every creature in this world, if humankind were to deeply examine themselves [and see], is created in an exquisite manner that indicates the greatness and power of a creator who created all of it. All of God's

103. The Holy Quran, 9:7-8.

104. 28 Rabi al-Awwal 1437 AH. From his advice to the youth. Source: [https://www.sistani.org/arabic/archive/25237]

prophetic messages were sent to remind us of this. Furthermore, God showed his servants that the reality of this life is that it is a test to see who has the best deeds at the end.

Whoever is incapable of truly realizing the presence of God and the afterlife will be deprived of understanding the meaning of life, its different dimensions, and its eventual end, and they will have no guiding lantern to point out how to traverse it. Therefore, each of you should protect this belief and preserve it firmly as your most prized possession, and strive to increase in certainty [of it] and keep it alive, flourishing and insightful so it is with you at all times. If a youth finds themselves in a moment of weakness in religion due to the vigor of age, like feeling neglectful towards obligations or experiencing temptation for vice, then they should not cut off from God all together because this will make returning to Him difficult.

Know that if a person knowingly neglects or rejects God during moments when they are feeling strong and well, arrogantly assuming invincibility, then God will make it so that they will have to turn to Him during their weakness and inability. So, in the moments of overwhelming self-confidence, which only last for a limited time, let them remember what is to come of inevitable weakness, incapacity, sickness, and old age.

They should never doubt the basic principles of belief just so they can justify their actions or behavior, which they were uncertain about and did not have enough patience to [deeply] examine. Nor should they follow their immediate desires and immature ideologies just because they seem appealing. Nor should they rely on immature thoughts, be deceived by the pleasures of this life, or develop resentment at the misappropriation of religion by certain people who use it for personal purposes. The truth is not measured by men, rather men are measured by the truth.[105]

Pearl 38: Adherence to virtuous actions and good character

I advise the youth about the necessity of upholding virtuous actions and avoiding vices. No happiness can be found without virtue, and all hardships, except those which are a test of God, are rooted in vices. God Almighty says, "Whatever hardship befalls you is the result of your own deeds. God pardons many of your sins."[106] These virtues include self-accountability, modesty in look and action, truthfulness in speech, connecting with the kin and relatives, fulfillment of trust and being true to covenants and commitments, strictness in adhering to the truth, and rising above despicable and ridiculous behaviors. On the other hand, the vices include harboring loathsome prejudices, hastiness in reaction, seeking pleasures that will cause degradation, showing off in front of others, extravagant spending when wealthy, rebelliousness in poverty, complacency during affliction, abuse of others, especially the weak, wastage of money, denial of blessings, pride in sin, aiding in injustice and aggression being prideful of sins, and pleasure at being unjustifiably praised. It is

---

105. 28 Rabi al-Awwal 1437 AH. From his advice to the youth. Source: [https://www.sistani.org/arabic/archive/25237]

106. The Holy Quran, 42:30.

necessary to embody the qualities of good-naturedness, which include wisdom, deliberateness, gentleness, modesty, prudence, tolerance, patience, and others, because these are all crucial to finding happiness in this life and the next. The closest people to God with the weightiest good deeds on the Day of Judgement are those with the best ethics and manners. Thus, be good in your treatment of your parents, family, children, friends, and people in general. If you find a deficiency in yourself, do not neglect it. Discipline and hold yourself accountable, and direct yourself wisely so you can fulfill your [God-given] purpose. However, if you find that there is an impediment that [seemingly] prevents you, do not despair. Instead, keep trying to embody goodness because the more you adopt the nature of virtuous people, the more you will actually become like them. Furthermore, the effort you put into attaining virtues you do not naturally possess is rewarded more by God than the effort of those who already possess these virtues in their nature.[107]

Pearl 39: Finding a profession and gaining skills

It is important for the youth that they achieve excellence in a profession and specialize in a field, and that they commit to their work and practice self-discipline and hard work because it will bring many blessings. This endeavor will occupy an amount of their time, it will be a source of earning for themselves and their family and they will benefit their community.

---

107. 28 Rabi al-Awwal 1437 AH. From his advice to the youth.
Source: [https://www.sistani.org/arabic/archive/25237].

Moreover, it will help them do good and gain skills that will sharpen their mind, enrich their experience and purify their wealth. The more a person must toil to earn their [halal] wealth the greater its purity and blessing for them. God loves a person who is hardworking in earning their living, and He despises those who are idle and are a burden upon others, or who spend all their time fooling around and having fun. Do not allow your youth to pass by without acquiring a skill or a profession because God gives people physical and mental vigor in their youth so they can use it to attain a skill that will benefit them for the rest of their life. So, do not waste your youth in trivialities and negligence.[108]

Pearl 40: Marriage and starting a family

The youth should give importance to starting a family by getting married and having children as soon as feasibly possible. Marriage brings pleasure and dignity to people and it becomes motivation to work hard and be responsible. It is an investment of one's energy and it protects them from many forbidden sins. This is why it has been narrated that "Whoever gets married has completed half of their religion."[109] Most importantly, marriage is a necessary *sunnah* and one that is greatly stressed during a person's life. It is a natural instinct in every human. If a person abstains from getting married, they put themselves at risk of succumbing to prohibitions and being afflicted with lethargy and laziness. A person should not be worried about the

---

108. 28 Rabi al-Awwal 1437 AH. From his advice to the youth. Source: [https://www.sistani.org/arabic/archive/25237]

109. Al-kulayni, *Al-kafi*, vol.5, p.329.

financial burden of marriage because God has made marriage a source of blessings, even if it is not evident at the beginning. More importantly, one should be concerned about the character of the person they are marrying, as well as their religion, and how they were raised. They should not focus on beauty/handsomeness, physical appearance, and their job because these will quickly fade away and reveal the true person underneath as life passes. We have many narrations that talk about the danger of marrying a woman for her appearance only. Lastly, a man should know that if he marries a woman for her religion and virtues, God will bless their marriage.[110]

Pearl 41: Benefitting others and striving for common good

I advise the youth to strive towards doing good, helping others, and striving for the common good, especially when it comes to the affairs of orphans, widows, and those in need. This will help strengthen faith, train the self, and give back the many blessings that have been received. It is a subtle way that promotes a virtuous society, cooperation amongst people, enjoining good, and forbidding evil, and it also helps the guardians of society preserve public order and promote the common good. It also helps uplift and advance the society. Doing good will bring blessings to one's life in this world and a great reward in the next. God loves a society in which individuals care about each other, wish good for each other, and are concerned about

---

110. 28 Rabi al-Awwal 1437 AH. From his advice to the youth. Source: [https://www.sistani.org/arabic/archive/25237]

each other's pain and problems. God Almighty says in the Holy Quran, "Had the people of the towns believed (in Our revelations) and maintained piety, We would have certainly showered on them Our blessings from the sky and the earth. But they called Our revelations lies, thus Our torment struck them for their evil deeds."¹¹¹ In another verse, God says, "Everyone is guarded and protected on all sides by the order of God. God does not change the condition of a nation unless it changes what is in its heart. When God wants to punish a people, there is no way to escape from it and no one besides God will protect them from it."¹¹² In addition, it has been narrated that the Prophet said, "A person is not a believer until they want for their brother/sister what they want for themselves and hate for their brother/sister what they hate for themselves."¹¹³ The Prophet Muhammad (pbuh&hp) also said, "Whoever plants a good deed (and is a role model of it), they will be rewarded for doing the deed and rewarded for everyone who [follows them] and does the deed."¹¹⁴ ¹¹⁵

111. The Holy Quran, 7:96.

112. The Holy Quran, 13:11.

113. Al-Shahid al-thani, *Muniyat al-mureed,* p.190.

114. Al-majlisi, *Bihar al-Anwar,* vol.74, p.164.

115. 28 Rabi al-Awwal 1437 AH. From his advice to the youth. Source: [https://www.sistani.org/arabic/archive/25237].

Guidelines for girls and young women

Pearl 42: Importance of modesty

I emphasize the importance of modesty for girls and young women. A girl, because of her nature, is more liable to suffer [negative] consequences if she is not cognizant of her modesty. She should not succumb to fake emotions or become involved in cursory relationships that bring momentary pleasure, but everlasting pain and repercussions. Thus, girls and young women should only concern themselves with establishing a healthy and stable life based on righteousness and happiness. A woman who has poise and confidence, preserves modesty in her clothing and actions, and is concerned only with her life, work, and studies, is the one who is truly honored.[116]

Pearl 43: Balance between work and nurturing a family

Women should not choose to advance their jobs at the expense of starting and caring for a family. Marriage is a strongly recommended practice in life whereas a job is supererogatory and [only] complementary to the essentials of life. Thus, it is not wise to leave the former for the latter. Anyone who is neglectful of this aspect of their youth may regret it later when it is already too

---

116. 28 Rabi al-Awwal 1437 AH. From his advice to the youth. Source: [https://www.sistani.org/arabic/archive/25237].

late. Many real-life experiences serve as a proof of this point.[117]

Pearl 44: Removing the obstacles to marriage

A woman's parents should not place obstacles and conditions in getting their daughter married, especially those conditions that God has not required in a marriage, such as outrageous dowries, or waiting for suitors from within the family or even a sayyid. Putting these obstacles and delaying marriage has negative and destructive consequences that the parents cannot fathom. Fathers should know that God established their guardianship over the daughters only so they may advise them of what is good and protective for them. Anyone who prevents a woman from a marriage that is good for her has committed a great sin and will suffer the consequences as long as she is hurt by it, and it is as if he has opened one of the gates of hell upon himself.[118]

---

117. 28 Rabi al-Awwal 1437 AH. From his advice to the youth. Source: [https://www.sistani.org/arabic/archive/25237].

118. 28 Rabi al-Awwal 1437 AH. From his advice to the youth. Source: [https://www.sistani.org/arabic/archive/25237].

Part Two

·············••◆••·············

Advice for the Islamic Seminary Teachers and Students of Religious Studies

Matters concerning teachers and educators

Pearl 45: Humility and respect

It is necessary for teachers and educators to be humble and respectful towards those they teach.[119]

Pearl 46: Consideration for students of knowledge

Teachers and educators should never embarrass their students or disparage them in any way. If they notice that the student has not understood what is being taught or the student makes a mistake, they should [subtly] point out and clarify the matter by raising a question, like, "what if it was such-and-such?" or "is there a chance the matter could be something other [than how you understand it]...?"[120]

Pearl 47: Prepare for class and research

Teachers and educators should advise their students to read and study the lessons before attending class. This improves their readiness, shortens the time required to learn, and focuses their attention so they do not have to rely entirely on the teacher's explanation

---

119. Wednesday, 17 Shawwal 1438 AH, from a confirmed and documented discourse by His Eminence to some scholars during a visit.

120. Ibid.

during class. This will allow the teacher to explain the points from the prior reading that they do not understand. The story of Shaykh Ahmad al-Ardabili with the two authors of "al-Madarik" and "al-Ma'alem" (may God give them distinction) is well-known,[121] and to this day, we still witness the importance and widespread usage of these two books despite the length of time and the fact that the author of "al-Ma'alem" has a more important book, "Muntaqa al-Jumman."[122]

Pearl 48: Adorn oneself with religious manners

It is necessary that teachers and educators conform to religious manners because it will create reverence for them in the hearts of the students and increase the

---

121. It is said that when Shaykh Hassan al-Ameli al-Jab'I (1011 AH) and Sayyid Muhammad al-Musawi al-Ameli al-Jab'i (1009 AH) came to the Holy City of Najaf from Lebanon seeking the knowledge of Ahl al-Bayt (p), they asked Shaykh Ahmad al-Ardabili (993 AH) to give them a private class, with the condition that he only explains his opinion if it is different for a particular ruling. He accepted. Thus, they silently read many rulings without anyone saying anything, such that some students mocked them. Shaykh al-Ardabili said to the students, "Soon, they will return to Mount Amel (Lebanon) and write many books, which you will read." It ended up like he said, they wrote many books that reached Iraq, which were read by many students. Shaykh Hassan became known by his book "Ma'alem al-Din" and was hereto forth called "Shaykh Hassan of the Ma'alem," while Sayyid Muhammad became known by his book "Madarek al-Ahkam fi Sharh Sharai' al-Islam" and was thereafter known as "Sayyid Muhammad of the Madarek."

122. Wednesday, 17 Shawwal 1438 AH, from a confirmed and documented discourse by His Eminence to some scholars during a visit.

impact of their words. I studied under many teachers in the sacred city of Mashhad[123] and the holy city of Najaf,[124] and each one of them had something which distinguished them from the others. Yet, the teacher who influenced me the most was Sayyid Mohsen al-Hakim (may God give him distinction).[125] I attended

---

123. Mashhad is the name given later to a large area consisting of several villages like Tus and Sanabad, east of the Khorasan region in Iran. It is known for its privilege of interring the body of Imam Ali Ibn Musa al-Rida (p). His noble shrine is located there and is visited by millions every year since his martyrdom in 303 AH.

124. An area in the back of Kufa, Iraq. It was built during the time of Imam Jafar Ibn Muhammad al-Sadiq (p)(148 AH) after revealing that it was the location of the grave of the Commander of the Faithful Ali Ibn Abi Taleb (40 AH). Since then, the area became the sanctuary of scholars and jurists to the extent that its reputation in intellect and knowledge covered the central city of Kufa, especially during the time of Imam al-Sadiq (p). It prospered and expanded, and its circles of knowledge became officially recognized when the author of the two most important narration sources from the Ahl al-Bayt (p), al-Istibsar and Tahthib al-Ahkam, Shaykh Muhammad Ibn al-Hassan al-Tusi (360 AH) who is known as "Shaykh al-Taifa" (Shaykh of the Sect). He migrated there following the invasion of the Seljuk Tughril Baig's army of Baghdad, where they burned the old libraries and demolished the house of Shaykh al-Tusi in the years 447-449 AH. As such, the Islamic Seminary of Najaf was established by him. Since then, the seminary has attracted students of knowledge from east and west, and has given rise to hundreds of jurists, philosophers, narrators, writers, and poets, despite suppression by tyrants and oppressive regimes.

125. Sayyid Muhsin al-Tabatabaei al-Hakim (1306-1390 AH) was one of the most prominent jurists of the seminary and the supreme religious authority for the Shia in his time. He is the author of "Mustamsak al-Urwah al-Wuthqa" which is considered one of the most important modern jurisprudential encyclopedias. He also had an influential role in the Cultural Shia Renaissance, confronting communism, and putting out sectarian conflicts

some of his lessons in the al-Khadhraa Mosque[126] and the Mosque of Imran[127] in Najaf, he was very careful in maintaining a religious decorum in his lessons, words, movements, and silence, and more precise in it than anyone else I knew. For example, he would enter the class quietly and tranquilly and then pray two units to greet the mosque while the students watched him. Then he would ascend the pulpit and give his lesson.[128]

Pearl 49: Revere the status of scholars

Teachers must be respectful when they mention the scholars and relate their opinions. I do not mean that they should unduly praise them, rather, they should respect and safeguard the status of the scholars. Thus, teachers should not be extravagant in praise, flattery,

---

between Muslims with his infamous Fatwa prohibiting the fighting of Kurds in Iraq.

126. It is considered one of the oldest mosques in Najaf. It is uncertain who founded it or why it is called al-Khadhraa (the Green). It is located on the eastern side of the holy shrine, to the right of the al-Sa'ah gate. It has two doors, one leads to the outside and the other leads inside the shrine through the second hall of the eastern wall. Many jurists have delivered their lessons, discussions, and prayers in it, like the jurist Sayyid Abul-Qassem al-Khoei, Sayyid al-Sistani, and others.

127. One of the oldest mosques of Najaf. It is attributed to the emir of the Batahites Imran Ibn Shahin (369 AH), it was built along with the re-construction of the holy Alawite shrine by Adud al-Dawla of the Buyids, which was completed in 371 AH. This mosque is located in the northern side of the shrine, to the right of the al-Tusi gate.

128. Wednesday, 17 Shawwal 1438 AH, from a confirmed and documented discourse by His Eminence to some scholars during a visit.

and giving lengthy titles, especially for living scholars. Instead, they should show reverence towards them and not demean them because that has a great effect in the minds of their students and their behavior later on.[129]

Pearl 50: How to Defend the Religious Authority

The best way to defend the religious authority against suspicions and misconceptions raised about it is by representing it through the practical work of scholars, and not necessarily by only writing rebuttals, even though the latter is important. In fact, any writing can be met with hundreds of written responses, but the effect of all these hundreds of writings can be countered in the minds of the people if they behold the example of even one true scholar who is committed to the principles he advocates and calls others towards.[130]

Pearl 51: Being knowledgeable and well-versed about the era in which one lives

A religious scholar must be knowledgeable about the era in which they live and immune from doubts to be influential and fulfill the role expected of them. It has been narrated that Sayyid Abul-Hassan al-Isfahani

---

129. Wednesday, 17 Shawal 1437 AH, from a confirmed and documented discourse by His Eminence to some scholars during a visit.

130. Sunday, 22 Jumada al-Ula 1435 AH, from a confirmed and documented discourse by His Eminence to some scholars during a visit.

(may God give him distinction)[131] said, "The sciences which establish the ability to interpret and derive authentic [jurisprudential] conclusions are one part of a hundred that are required for a person to become a jurist."[132]

Pearl 52: Affirming love and peaceful coexistence

One of the most important duties of religious and spiritual leaders is the affirmation of love and peaceful coexistence, which are built on the protection of rights and mutual respect between followers of different religions and intellectual approaches.[133]

Matters concerning students of the Islamic seminaries

Pearl 53: Earnestness and effort in study

I advise myself and you to be earnest and give effort in your studies, and to not be concerned with people and

---

131. Sayyid Abul-Hassan al-Isfahani (1284-1365 AH), a senior Shia jurist, and the grand religious authority for the Shia in his time. He has many respectable political stances, such as his stance against the British occupation of Iraq.

132. Sunday, 22 Jumada al-Ula 1435 AH, from a confirmed and documented discourse by His Eminence to some scholars during a visit.

133. 25 Safar 1425 AH, Source: [https://www.sistani.org/arabic/statement/1491] and 29 Ramadan 1431 AH, Source: [https://www.sistani.org/arabic/statement/1513]

their views of you. Instead, your concern and goal should be to gain the satisfaction of Imam Mahdi (may God hasten his return).[134]

Pearl 54: Acquiring deep religious understanding and serving the believers

Fear God and be vigilant about obtaining religious knowledge. Fear God and be vigilant when you engage the believers to fulfill your religious duty. Strive to bring good tidings and warnings of God's mercy to them, and in doing so, support Imam Mahdi (may God hasten his return). The Imam is beleaguered because the Shia are occupied with their money and families and have abandoned him and are unprepared to support him.[135]

Pearl 55: Satisfying Imam Mahdi (may God hasten his return)

Fear God and be vigilant in preparing yourself, your family, and all those around you to serve and support Imam Mahdi (may God hasten his return). Strive to gain the satisfaction of your Imam.[136]

---

134. Wednesday, 29 Jumada al-Ula 1436 AH, from a confirmed and documented discourse by His Eminence to some scholars during a visit.

135. Ibid.

136. Wednesday, 17 Shawwal 1437 AH, from a confirmed and documented discourse by His Eminence to some scholars during a visit.

Pearl 56: Struggle of the Self

I advise the students of religious studies to focus on reading the book *Jihad al-Nafs* (Struggle of the Soul) from *Wasail al-Shia*,[137] and to read the books that relate the beauty of the Prophet and Ahl al-Bayt's words because they affect the hearts, like *Nahj al-Balaghah* (Peak of Eloquence),[138] *Tuhaf al-Uqul* (Masterpeices of the Mind)[139] and others.

Pearl 57: The importance of preserving the status and criteria of being a student of knowledge

It is necessary for students of knowledge to preserve the status and criteria that distinguish them as seekers of knowledge, even in the way they live and behave, the nature of their family, and their interactions with others. People hold scholars in a very high and noble status, and they trust in them as a reliable source.

---

137. Al-Wasail, the abbreviation for "Tafsil Wasail al-Shia Ila Tahsil Masail al-Shariah" (The Detailed Sources of the Shia for Obtaining Rulings of Islamic Law) by Shaykh Muhammad Ibn al-Hassan Ibn Ali, known as Shaykh Hurr al-Ameli (1104 AH). The book is one of the most important encyclopedias and collections of narrations from the Imams of Ahl al-Bayt (p) in jurisprudence.

138. This book is a number of selected sermons, letters, and quotes by Imam Ali (p). They have been gathered together in one book by the jurist and writer, Sayyid Muhammad bin al-Hussain, known as al-Sharif al-Radi. (406 AH).

139. "Tuhaf al-Uqul fi ma jaa' min al-Hikam wa al-Mawa'idh 'aan al-Rasul" (Masterpieces of the Mind in What Came of Wisdom and Exhortations from the Family of the Messenger), written by Abi Shu'ba al-Harrani, a Shia scholar from Aleppo in the fourth century AH.

Therefore, the student should preserve this image by strengthening their desire to call others to God and the hereafter and turn away from this life, and avoid calling people to themselves. If a student sincerely looks towards the hereafter [as the true abode], they will have a great effect on the people and they will be able to correct their thoughts and trajectories in life. However, if they only look towards this life and draw attention to themselves, then this will corrupt the beliefs of the people and create doubt in their minds about their religion. I remember when I was in the city of Mashhad, I knew some pious traders, who would say, "We aren't people of knowledge or those who read books about belief like Tajrid al-Iitiqad,[140] but our faith is true and correct because we know scholars like Shaykh Hussain al-Qummi and others in whom we observed asceticism, piety, and rejection of the world, which had a profound effect on our minds and adherence to the religion and faith".[141]

---

140. "Tajrid al-Itiqad" (the Purification of the Belief) is a specialist book in theology and doctrine, and the elements that relate to the fundamentals of religion. It is written by Shaykh Nasir al-Din al-Tusi (672), the philosopher and astronomical mathematician who established the Maraghah Observatory during the Mongol invasion. Many scholars have explained and commented on the book, notably his student Shaykh Hassan Ibn al-Mutahhar, known as Allamah al-Hilli (726 AH) in his book "Kashf al-Murad fi Sharh Tajrid al-Itiqad" (Unveiling the Meaning in Commentary on the Purification of the Belief), which is considered one of the most important and trustworthy educational texts in the seminaries today.

141. Wednesday, 17 Shawwal 1438 AH, from a confirmed and documented discourse by His Eminence to some scholars during a visit.

Pearl 58: Concern for scholarly titles

The student should not seek titles like Allamah,
Ayatollah, Marja, etc. or for people to kiss his hand or
to unduly respect him. This is worthless without
sincerity. Imagine, even the master of this dome (i.e.,
shrine), the Commander of the Faithful (p), has often
been undervalued and even cursed and insulted on the
pulpits of his enemies. Yet, will come to know his
position with God Almighty and His Messenger (p), and
today we can see his shining dome, and in contrast, the
graves of his enemies.[142]

Pearl 59: Preachers are callers to God, His Messenger, and the Imams

The duty of an Islamic preacher is to call others to the
fundamentals of religion and to spread its tenets and
immutable teachings, which are represented in the
verses of the Honorable Book and the poignant words
of the Prophet (p) and guiding Imams (p). They must
warn and guide the people to increase their faith in God
Almighty, prepare themselves for the Day of Judgement,
strive to purify and train themselves against evil traits
and shameful characteristics, beautify themselves with
honorable morals and praiseworthy traits, and improve
their treatment of others, even those who oppose them
in religion and faith.[143]

---

142. Wednesday, 29 Jumada al-Ula 1436 AH, from a confirmed and
documented discourse by His Eminence to some scholars during a
visit.

143. 9 Jumada al-Akhir 1440 AH, Fatwa. Source:
[https://www.sistani.org/arabic/archive/26261]

Pearl 60: The impact of the beautiful words of Ahl al-Bayt (p)

The beautiful words of Ahl al-Bayt (p) should be spread for their beneficial impact on people. It has been narrated that Imam al-Rida (p) said, "Indeed, if people knew the significance of our words, they would follow us."[144] Therefore, this should be given importance, and the words of the infallible Imams should be clarified and explained because most people do not have the ability to understand everything that has been narrated from them.[145]

---

144. Al-Majlisi, Bihar al-Anwar, vol.2, p.30.

145. Wednesday, 29 Jumada al-Ula 1436 AH, from a confirmed and documented discourse by His Eminence to some scholars during a visit.

Part Three

········•◆•········

Advice Concerning Hussaini Lectures and Speakers

It may not be an exaggeration to say that the events of Karbala, and what has been narrated from the Imams of the Ahl al-Bayt about its importance, the necessity of its commemoration and participation in its rituals, and its presence in the minds and hearts of the believers throughout history, makes it one of the most important Islamic occasions and religious ceremonies. It has had and continues to have a significant impact on society and politics throughout history, and it plays an important role in educating the masses because it spreads knowledge, promotes engagement, and cultivates the character by taking a stance against injustice and those who strive to oppress others. Thus, the Hussaini tradition has become one of the main landmarks of Islam and Muslims in the current age.

As a result, and as is patently clear, it was necessary for the religious and spiritual leadership to preserve and maintain the rituals, safeguard them from harm, and to prevent the enemies from usurping its hidden power and its significance in the hearts of people. These pearls provide direction and guidance and remind of the importance of the Hussaini tradition, which must continue, and describe the qualities and characteristics of the Hussaini pulpit, as well as those who commemorate, whether they are a speaker, preacher, reciter, or the organizers of mourning ceremonies, gatherings, or Hussaini processions.

The importance of the period of mourning for Imam Hussain (p)

Pearl 61: Our repository of religious heritage

The gatherings and commemorations for the Master of Martyrs and the demonstrations of mourning, which the believers have inherited from their forefathers, are the greatest heritage that we must preserve with all of our abilities and never neglect. We have seen how it has inspired our youth and even our elderly to come out en masse with great courage and bravery to defend the honor of this tradition, the sacred places, and everything that is holy by writing the most beautiful of epics, all of which will be immortalized by history. This beneficial result is enough reason to maintain these gatherings.[146]

Pearl 62: The necessity of loving and showing your love for the Prophet and his household

It is our duty as believers and by virtue of what God has engrained in our consciences and instilled in our natures to love those who do good to us. In addition, He has commanded us to love the Prophet and his Household (p) more than we love for our fathers, mothers, offspring and all of our relatives. Are they not the people through whom God's greatest blessing, His guidance to faith, came through? This is the same love

---

146. 5 Muharram 1438 AH. Friday Sermon. Source: [https://www.sistani.org/arabic/archive/25477]

for God, which is described as the essence of religion in the holy script.[147]

Pearl 63: Grief is a sign of true love and loyalty

There is no doubt that sorrow over the suffering of the Master of the Martyrs (p) is a true representation of love and loyalty to the Prophet of this *ummah* and his purified family who God has chosen and commanded us to love. This love is a reward for the message conveyed by the Prophet, as God Almighty says, "Say, I do not ask you for a reward for this message only love for kinship."[148] The noble narrations from the Prophet (p) have explained that this "kinship" refers to Ali and Fatima, and their children al-Hasan and al-Hussain.[149]

Pearl 64: Mourning in the Hussaini gatherings (majalis)

Mourning and remembering the suffering of Ahl al-Bayt (p), especially during the days of the month of Muharram, are a foundation of majalis. The hearts of the believers become fearful of God by it and His blessings descend and strengthen their faith, firm their

---

147. Ibid

148. The Holy Quran, 42:23.

149. 5 Muharram 1438 AH. Friday Sermon. Source: [https://www.sistani.org/arabic/archive/25477]

conviction, and drive them towards performing acts of kindness and good.[150]

Pearl 65: The message of the Hussaini pulpit

In addition to relating the calamities and struggles that befell the Ahl al-Bayt, it is important to remember that the essential role of the pulpit is to spread the religion and establish it in the minds and hearts of Muslims through Quranic knowledge, dispel doubts with comprehensive and persuasive proofs, and nurturing piety, virtue, and moral values in the believers. This is precisely the role that God Almighty gave to His Messenger who was the first to ascend the pulpit of Islam. The Quran has explained to us this role, "It is He who has sent among the illiterates a Messenger from themselves reciting to them His verses and purifying them and teaching them the Book and wisdom, for indeed they had previously been clearly astray."[151] The holy verse indicates that the message of the Prophet focuses on establishing the religion by purifying the self and cleansing it of the filth of darkness and spiritual and moral diseases. Moreover, it conveys Quranic insights and plants wisdom in the hearts through various means knowledge and practical guidance. Likewise, the lofty goal of the reformatory movement of the Master of Martyrs (p) was to preserve the religion and establish it as an opponent to the Umayyad way, which was founded on destroying the pillars and values of Islam, as can been seen in many

---

150. 27 Dhul-Hijjah 1440 AH. Statement Regarding Muharram 1441. Source: [https://www.sistani.org/arabic/archive/26341]

151. The Holy Quran, 62:2.

accounts. His uprising was established to
that dangerous way. His legacy and sacrifice
greater goal, which is to preserve the religion
rioration and deviation. I believe that if it was
not for the sacrifice of Imam al-Hussain (p) in that
great manner and through such adversity, there would
not be any trace of Islam left because the Umayyad plot
was shrewdly devised and had nearly accomplished its
objectives. Hence, because the Hussaini pulpit is an
extension of al-Hussain today, its role and function
must revolve around establishing, defending, and
educating people about the religion.[152]

Pearl 66: Demonstration of grief is a necessity

Demonstrations of grief and sorrow for the suffering of
the Master of the Youth of Paradise are very important
in the school of Ahl al-Bayt (p). Many traditions from
the Imams have indicated that crying for al-Hussain
and displaying grief for his suffering is a worship in itself,
it brings a believer closer to God and His Messenger and
has a great reward. It is narrated from Imam al-
Baqir (p) from his father Imam Zain al-Abideen (p) that
he said, "Any believer whose eyes shed a tear until it
rolls down their cheeks for what befell us of harm from
our enemy in this world, God will choose for them an
abode of sincerity (in the afterlife)."[153] It has also been
narrated that Imam al-Sadiq (p) would supplicate in his

---

152. 11 Dhul-Hijjah 1439 AH. Advice for Speakers and Preachers
Regarding the month of Muharram 1440. Source:
[https://www.sistani.org/arabic/archive/26110]

153. Ibn Qawlawiya, Jafar Ibn Mohammad, Kamel al-Ziyarat, p.201.

prostration, "O' Allah, have mercy on those cheeks that lamented over the grave of Abu Abdullah, and have mercy on those eyes that shed tears out of true remorse for us, and have mercy on those hearts which were anxious and burning for us, and have mercy on those cries that were for us."[154] [155]

Pearl 67: The signs of grief and its conditions

Spreading the emblems of Ashura by raising flags and black banners in yards, roadways, streets, and other public places, while simultaneously respecting private property, strengthens the commemoration of the legacy of Ahl al-Bayt (p) along with the majalis. This must be conducted with full consideration and adherence to the laws of the country, and through the internet and modern means of communication. It should include the sayings of Imam Hussain (p) from his great movement of reformation and what has been said about the tragedy of Karbala in the extraordinary poetry and prose.[156]

Pearl 68: Self-control and respecting others

The religious authority calls upon the believers to observe the highest standards of self-control while commemorating the mournful occasions and expressing passionate emotions towards what their Imams faced

---

154. Al-Majlisi, Bihar al-Anwar, vol.98, p.8.

155. 5 Muharram 1438 AH, Friday Sermon. Source: [https://www.sistani.org/arabic/archive/25477]

156. 9 Dhul-Hijjah 1441 AH. Source: [https://www.sistani.org/arabic/archive/26453]

of violations and aggression and to not say or do anything that disrespects our brothers of Ahl al-Sunna who are against those horrible crimes and will never accept it.[157]

What the Hussaini Majalis and Speeches Should Encompass and Address

Pearl 69: Topics from the Holy Quran

Speeches should focus on the Holy Quran and give it great importance because it is the message of God to all His creation, the weighty source in this ummah, and the balance of justice and injustice. God Almighty has revealed it as a guidance, light, and proof for the people, and it is a wise and holy message. The lives of the Ahl al-Bayt (p) and their sacrifices were an implementation of its teachings and in compliance with it. Therefore, it must be the primary message and source of discourse, and anything else that is mentioned should be under its domain and significance.[158]

Pearl 70: The fundamentals of faith

Speeches should include content that affirms the true fundamentals of faith and its clear proofs, which are strong and heartfelt, using simple and understandable

157. 23 Muharram 1428 AH. Source:
[https://www.sistani.org/arabic/statement/1505]

158. 27 Dhul-Hijjah 1440 AH. Statement Regarding Muharram 1441. Source: [https://www.sistani.org/arabic/archive/26341]

approaches. It should be presented as it has been in the Noble Quran, *sunnah* of the Prophet, and narrations of the purified progeny, so that it becomes engrained in the minds of the people, any suspicions or doubts about it are removed and any assumed weaknesses of its tradition and doctrine are refuted. This can be achieved by reminding people of the proofs of God Almighty's existence, like the beauty of the universe and the marvels of His creation which are witnessed through human insight, advancements, and scientific facts. In addition, the speaker can discuss the evidence that points to the truth of the Prophet and the righteousness of this message using what has been revealed in the Holy Quran and verified throughout history. The preacher must remind the listeners of the afterlife and its importance, when every person will be brought with their book of deeds from this world and the balance of equity will be set on the Day of Judgement. On that day, every person will reap what they sowed of characteristics and deeds, and those who did wrong will answer for what they did and those who did good will receive good. The preacher should also mention examples from the Quran and valuable sayings of the Prophet and his progeny that are relevant to these circumstances. For example, the sermons of the Commander of Faithful in Nahj al-Balaghah,[159] which are a great example of what a speech should contain. He begins with the remembrance of God and His signs in creation, then he reminds the people of God's great right on them and His blessings

---

159. This book is a number of selected sermons, letters, and quotes by Imam Ali (p). They have been gathered together in one book by the jurist and writer, Sayyid Muhammad bin al-Hussain, known as al-Sharif al-Radi. (406 AH).

upon them. He then describes the message of the
Prophet and what it contains of guidance and meanings,
and then the afterlife in such a way that the listener
can visualize it. He also reminds of the status and
distinction of Ahl al-Bayt in this ummah. He also
mentions aspects of wisdom and virtue, which increase
righteousness and aid in nurturing social well-being.
Of course, there are different levels to the speech
depending on the requirements of the situation. Finally,
the supplications of al-Sahifa al-Sajjadiyah are a great
example of what the preacher can use in the end of
their speech by reciting a section of it to remind the
people of the eloquent prayers of the Imams.[160]

Pearl 71: Innate and lofty teachings and values

It is important for speeches to explain the divinely
bestowed innate human teachings and values portrayed
in the example of the Prophet and his progeny, and in
their lives and practices, and to clarify their position as
perfect role models to emulate. The Prophet and the
chosen members of his progeny are the banners of
guidance and the highest examples of this ummah in
their embodiment of the teachings of the Holy Quran
and its inherent values in terms of attachment to
God and His worship, and perfection in reasoning,
righteousness, and wisdom. In addition, they exemplify
the values of morality like justice, truth, kindness,
fulfillment of pledges, piety, virtue, and high ethics.
This is because they pledged themselves to this divine

160. 27 Dhul-Hijjah 1440 AH. Statement Regarding Muharram
1441. Source: [https://www.sistani.org/arabic/archive/26341]

cause and sacrificed their lives for it. Thus, it is necessary to expound upon the principles of these teachings and values through the Holy Quran, which is complimented by their beautiful sayings, honorable morals, and their lives until their martyrdom, particularly as it applies to modern times. This is the true way of showing their personalities and the goals which they sacrificed while they fulfilled the divine call for God Almighty. God Almighty has made the chosen ones of each nation the examples to the rest of its members, the models to its people, and the proof upon those who fell behind. He said about Jesus son of Mary (p), "And We made him an example to Children of Israel."[161] As the Prophet and his progeny were a proof on the ummah and an example for it. God said, "Indeed, in the Messenger of Allah you have an excellent example for whoever has hope in Allah and the Final Day, and remembers Allah often."[162] It has been narrated that the Commander of Faithful (p) said in a message to one of his governors after describing his asceticism of this world, "You cannot do so (i.e., live like me), but at least support me in piety, effort, virtue and righteousness."[163] So, speakers and preachers should emphasize righteousness, wisdom, and morality in the sayings and lives of the infallibles. They should examine them and focus on clarifying their meaning, and call for awareness about them. They should exhort the people to follow them and set them as an example

---

161. The Holy Quran, 43:59.

162. The Holy Quran, 33:21.

163. Al-Sharif al-Radi, Nahj al-Balagha, Book of Letters, Letter 45 to Uthman Ibn Hunayf

in a manner suitable with the present time. Poets should strive to include the virtuous, wise, and lofty elements that foster the mind, awaken the conscience, increase righteousness, and drive people to follow the Book of God and the tradition of His Prophet and his purified progeny in their poetry about Ahl al-Bayt. This is the appropriate way of presenting the lives of the Imams, their sacrifices, and what happened to them because eloquent poetry has a strong effect on the minds and a tremendous ability to ignite emotions. Therefore, it should be benefited from in the best way to achieve righteous and noble objectives.[164]

Pearl 72: The Ahl al-Bayt's specific directives to their followers and lovers

After the Holy Quran, it is important that the content of speeches covers the specific directives of Ahl al-Bayt to their followers and lovers. It should be explained to the public because the Imams of Ahl al-Bayt have advice and guidance meant for their lovers and followers, in addition to their explanations of religious rulings, commandments to all Muslims, and their affirmation of the importance of recognizing the position of Ahl al-Bayt amongst the ummah and the unique status given to them by God. It is important to share these directives with Muslims so that they can learn and adopt their manners and entrench it in their customs. These directives emphasize a practical commitment to the teachings of their religion, having love for each other, and striving to live by their traits

---

164. 27 Dhul-Hijjah 1440 AH. Statement Regarding Muharram 1441. Source: [https://www.sistani.org/arabic/archive/26341]

and honorable manners, even with people of different religions and sects, aside from those with the same views. As Imam Abu Abdullah al-Sadiq says, "You must have fear of God and be cognizant of Him, strive with effort, be truthful in your speech, be trustworthy, have good manners, and be good to your neighbor. Be callers to good without your tongues (i.e., by your actions), and be an adornment (for us) and not a disgrace."[165] Also, in a narration by Jabir al-Jufi that Abu Jafar al-Baqir said, "Tell me O' Jabir, do people think that just claiming to be our Shia and saying they love us (Ahl al-Bayt) is enough? I swear by Allah, our Shia are only those who are pious before Allah and obey Him. O' Jabir, no one will know them except by their humility, piety, trustworthiness, constant remembrance of Allah, fasting, prayer, righteousness towards parents, good relations with neighbors, the poor, the needy, the indebted, and the orphans, and by their truthfulness of speech, recitation of the Quran, restraining their tongues except for good, and they are the trustees of their tribes."[166] He also said, "O' Jabir, do not allow sectarianism to confuse you. Does a person think that saying 'I love Ali and support him' without being implementing his way is enough? Moreover, if one says they love the Messenger of Allah, and the Messenger of Allah is better than Ali, but they do not follow his way of life or practice his tradition, their love will be of no benefit. Therefore, fear God and work for what is with God. There is no family relation between any person and God, instead, the most beloved person to God

---

165. Al-Majlisi, Bihar al-Anwar, vol.67, p.299.

166. Al-Kulayni, al-Kafi, vol.2, p.74.

Almighty of His servants and the most noble in His eyes are the most pious and obedient to Him. O' Jabir, by Allah, nothing brings one nearer to Allah Almighty except obedience, no one is immune from hellfire, and no one has any argument over Allah. Whoever is obedient to Allah is our supporter, and whoever is disobedient to Allah is our enemy. Our guardianship is not acquired except through pious work."[167] In a narration from Muawiyah Ibn Wahab, he said, "I asked him, 'How should we deal with our own people and those we associate with of the people who are not on our way?" Abu Abdullah al-Sadiq (p) said, 'Look at your Imams whom you follow and do as they do. By Allah, they visit their sick, participate in their funerals, present their testimony for and against them, and faithfully discharge their trust."[168] In another narration, "The easiest way of making people pleased with you is by restraining your tongues from (attacking) them."[169] [170]

Pearl 73: Avoiding what causes division and difference

Speeches must avoid anything that will cause division and difference between the believers, and instead, give importance to maintaining unity, cooperation, and love for one another. This is achieved by avoiding any topics that emphasize the differences between them,

167. Ibid.

168. Al-Kulayni, al-Kafi, vol.2, p.626.

169. Al-Kulayni, al-Kafi, vol.8, p.341.

170. 27 Dhul-Hijjah 1440 AH. Statement Regarding Muharram 1441. Source: [https://www.sistani.org/arabic/archive/26341]

like the differences in emulation and some of the varying opinions of the jurists on certain issues. This includes every disagreement that does not cause some of them to deviate from the Book or progeny, even if it is due to differences in the degrees of faith, vision, commitment, or righteousness, or even if it was from a misstep by a certain person. Furthermore, the mistake should not be announced or made public because defaming its doer will cause it to spread further and may cause them to persist along with those who are influenced by them. This weakens the truth, which must be preserved, irrespective of the fact that it is impermissible to defame a believer and denigrate them for a mistake, especially if doing so gives an incorrect impression of them that does not consider all of their other characteristics and merits. A mistake may subside with silence and not mentioning it, while speaking of it and explaining it could ignite it. Thus, silence in regard to something may be better than speech. Beware of charging someone of faith with disbelief through [false] interpretation, suspicion, or saying something about their religion after a clear profession of faith, or that they do not belong to the school of Ahl al-Bayt after their clear acquiescence to their status in this ummah like the selection of the families of the Prophets in the previous nations for Imamate, judgement and knowledge. Whoever does so, contradicts the manners of the Ahl al-Bayt (p) and splits the lines of their supporters and followers, and commits a great mistake. Anything that causes division between the Muslims and triggers hatred and mistrust must be avoided. Doing so contradicts their teachings and manners because they made sure to treat others with good manners and they did not highlight people's differences in a manner that weakens Islam or distorts the truth. It has even been commanded to pray with them, defend them, and attend their gatherings and funerals. This is a confirmed and clear matter in history which can be seen in their traditions and ways. They were well-respected and praised by others, to the extent that they cared about learning and gaining from them. Avoiding matters like this does not require one to renounce their true faith or abandon their opposition and disassociation from those who oppressed them, nor does it require ignoring their oppression and not speaking of it because there are many ways of expounding a topic and fulfilling it in accordance with the situation. A wise speaker who is experienced in different ways of discourse and means of explanation should choose the appropriate style for the situation, just like the Imams did. For this reason, it has been narrated that they urged the scholars of their companions to learn the subtlety of their speech, which was what truly exemplified the meaning of what they were saying. It has been narrated that Imam al-Sadiq (p) said, "We do not consider a man from you to deeply understand until he knows our approach in speaking"[171] or "and one of you is not considered to have deep understanding until he knows the subtleties of our speech."[172] Preachers should avoid asking the public to judge or draw conclusions about theoretical and specialized matters which they are not responsible for because doing so builds a shallow understanding of the matter, allows the pretenders of knowledge and the

---

171. Al-Majlisi, Bihar al-Anwar, vol.2, p.208.

172. Al-Majlisi, Bihar al-Anwar, vol.2, p.184.

people of misguidance to use it, takes away the balance of knowledge, and weakens specialized understanding and those who have achieved it. Hence, it has very large negative side effects among the believers in the short and long term.[173]

Pearl 74: Presenting a variety of topics

It is best for speakers to present a variety of topics. The community needs spiritual, educational, and historical information. Therefore, the speaker should be able to explain various topics in several fields to cover some of the needs of those who have gathered to seek guidance and others.[174]

Pearl 75: Using contemporary language and culture

It is necessary for speeches to be contemporary with the culture of the time and the needs of the language and customs of the audience. This means that they should address the doubts about religion raised in every circumstance and the changing behaviors of believers in every community and time. Keeping abreast of new ideas, behavior or culture promotes

---

173. 27 Dhul-Hijjah 1440 AH. Statement Regarding Muharram 1441. Source: [https://www.sistani.org/arabic/archive/26341]

174. 23 Dhul-Hijjah 1437 AH. Advice for Speakers and Preachers Regarding the month of Muharram 1438. Source: [https://www.sistani.org/arabic/archive/25463]

support for the Husseini pulpit and keeps it alive and renewed, and greatly effective.[175]

Pearl 76: The Religious Authority and Islamic Seminary

It is important for the speech to remind of the importance of the religious authority, the Islamic seminary, and the scholarly foundation [of religion], which are the secret to the power of the Imami sect and a symbol of its greatness and the loftiness of its institution and structure.[176]

Pearl 77: Keeping the speech free of dreams and imagination

The speech should be free from relaying dreams and imaginary stories that will bring disrespect to the reputation of the Hussaini pulpit and make it seem like a medium that is incompatible with intellectual discourse and the appropriate level of understanding of the audience.[177]

Pearl 78: Social Problems and Solutions

The speech should discuss common social problems along with successful solutions. It is better for the speaker not to limit their speech to only presenting problems, such as the problems that cause family

---

175. Ibid.

176. Ibid.

177. Ibid.

breakdown, create a gap between the youth and the older generation, divorce, and others without presenting proportional solutions because this causes disputes without a contribution from the pulpit for an effective change. Therefore, it is desired that speakers of the Hussaini pulpit consult experts in social administration, psychology and sociology in determining successful solutions for the various problems so that every discourse includes a viable and beneficial solution, which will transform the pulpit from inactivity to a state of interaction, innovation, and leadership in reforming communities and improving them.[178]

Pearl 79: Avoiding involvement in domestic conflicts

The Hussaini discourse should transcend and avoid involvement in Shia conflicts, whether it is due to intellectual or ritual matters because doing so will create bias towards one group over another, will result in social chaos, or will cause a schism between the believers. Instead, the pulpit is a banner for unity and a symbol of the Hussaini light which unites the hearts of the lovers of the Master of Martyrs. It is one path and it represents effective cooperation.[179]

Pearl 80: Contributing to the period of Hussaini commemoration

The majalis of the Master of Martyrs and the great crowd of believers which it gathers is an opportunity

---

178. Ibid.

179. Ibid.

to educate the people in the matters of their faith, provide them with insight about their time, and give appropriate solutions to their intellectual problems.[180]

Necessary Qualities of Preachers, Speakers, Poets and Reciters

Pearl 81: Being fearful and sincere to God

It is necessary to embody fear of God and sincerity towards Him in speech, action and behavior before anything else. One should place God before their eyes, remember that He is ever watchful, strive for His pleasure and acceptance, and intend every act only for Him. God will awaken those who are sincere in fulfilling His right and fear Him in times of heedlessness. He will alert them during negligence and ease their path towards righteousness. Then He will bless their actions in this life and the next.[181]

Pearl 82: The Infallibles are witnesses over the people of knowledge

Preachers should know that the Prophet and his family are witnesses over them, the people of religious knowledge, and those who call others to religion in what they have fulfilled of this responsibility. Moreover, the people of knowledge are witnesses over

180. 5 Muharram 1438 AH, Friday Sermon. Source: [https://www.sistani.org/arabic/archive/25477]

181. 27 Dhul-Hijjah 1440 AH. Statement Regarding Muharram 1441. Source: [https://www.sistani.org/arabic/archive/26341]

others in their community in what they have performed and fulfilled. God Almighty said, "So that the Messenger may be a witness over you, and that you may be witnesses over humanity."[182] Therefore, anyone who is careless about the matter of preaching, whether in a saying or action, has no excuse and is burdened with it. On the other hand, whoever fulfills it but the people neglect what they have said or done is excused and is safe from punishment and reproach. Therefore, this is a serious matter for those who truly contemplate and understand its gravity.[183]

Pearl 83: Practice what you preach

Preachers must make their characteristics match their sayings and what they describe to others of lofty values. Thus, they should precede others in adopting and acting according to them because this will indicate sincerity and reject merely showing off in front of others. Moreover, it will foster sincerity in the audience and have a more profound effect. How can a person sincerely expound upon the characteristics of the Prophet and his noble family, like obedience to God, turning away from this world, and observing justice, truth, virtue, loyalty, kindness to parents, and the rest of the noble characteristics, and advice others to follow it, while not living it themselves? God Almighty said, "Do you preach righteousness and fail

---

182. The Holy Quran, 22:78.

183. 27 Dhul-Hijjah 1440 AH. Statement Regarding Muharram 1441. Source: [https://www.sistani.org/arabic/archive/26341]

to practice it yourselves,"[184] and, "O believers! Why do you say what you do not do?"[185]

Pearl 84: The impermissibility and danger of speaking without knowledge

Avoid speaking without knowledge and understanding because it is impermissible in religion, regardless of the speech's content. The Almighty said, "And do not pursue what you have no knowledge of; surely hearing and beholding and heart-sight, all of those will be questioned of."[186] A person's good intention and the legitimacy of the objective does not validate it, nor does it protect from its dangers and side-effects. It only becomes permissible with the development of a person's knowledge about the topic and an understanding of the details related to its establishment, rejection, conditions, certainty, doubt and when to act with precaution concerning it. This includes matters of history, its events, circumstances, and sources and their reliability. In general, the preacher should also be knowledgeable in the other religious sciences related to the subject. In addition, they should be well-prepared with the required tools, experienced in the topic of discourse, well-informed about the related details, and cautious about anything they do not know or have yet to learn. They should be very careful about creating innovations in religion or adding to it anything that is not a part of it or has no reliable proof, because doing so is one of

---

184. The Holy Quran, 2:44.

185. The Holy Quran, 61:2.

186. The Holy Quran, 17:36.

the most harmful kinds of misguidance. It leads to disparities in the understanding of religion and the formation of several belief systems, and the division of its people into varying and different groups. This is what has been observed in many religions and sects. The Prophet has warned of heresy, "The most evil matter is false innovation. Every innovation (i.e., falsely added element to religion) is a misguidance, and every misguidance leads to hell."[187]

Pearl 85: Avoiding sectarian conflicts and focusing on unity

There is no doubt that everyone is aware of the importance of coming together, refraining from division, and avoiding the incitement of sectarian conflicts. These conflicts have continued for centuries and it seems there is no solution that is accepted and pleases everyone. One should not promote debates about these matters, except in the realm of purely academic discussions. Thus, it is very important to focus on Islamic unity, especially since these discussions would not concern the principles of religion and tenets of faith (i.e., because we are all in agreement about them).[188] Those eager to elevate Islam and contribute to the advancement of Muslims should do everything in their power to bring Muslims closer together and minimize the tensions caused by certain political

187. Al-Majlisi, Bihar al-Anwar, vol.31, p.281.

188. 14 Muharram 1428. Source:
[https://www.sistani.org/arabic/statement/1504]

quarrels to prevent further division and not give any opportunity for the fulfillment of the enemy's goals.[189]

Pearl 86: Beware of exaggeration

Preachers should be careful about exaggerating and exceeding limits when they speak. Like developing a theoretical opinion, which requires advanced knowledge and effort to derive, and making it seem rudimentary or making a matter of disagreement among the scholars seem agreed upon, whether explicitly or implicitly, and thereby reduces its significance, or presenting something that is doubtful as verified, or something that is probable seem impossible. Moreover, they should not raise some religious duties to a status above what they really are, like placing a recommended act at the status of an obligatory act without connecting its significance as a auxiliary element of some other obligatory act, or a non-fundamental obligatory act in place of one that is fundamental, or vice-versa. All of this is religiously unacceptable. A person who occupies an educational and nurturing role among the people, and affiliates with the Imams of Ahl al-Bayt to provide education and training should refrain from this. Surely, there is no good in speech without vigilance or discourse without piety, and whoever fears God Almighty, it is better for them and safer in what they seek. One should avoid speaking without knowledge while being cautious in presenting narrations and events, and they should confirm the matter by fully reading and understanding it several times before speaking about it. Hence, no word will come out of them without a thorough

---

189. Ibid.

comprehension of it. They should remind themselves that there is no way to recant or withdraw something erroneous after delivering a speech in public. More importantly, not saying what should not be said is better than having to apologize for it or attempt to clarify it later. Preachers should also be careful about arguing a truthful point using falsehood because that weakens the truth and creates confusion. It is clear that confirmation of the truth and the evidence that points to it does not need false proofs.[190]

Pearl 87: Personalizing the pulpit and the duty of the believers

It is not appropriate for a speaker to present specialized research topics to the public which they are not familiar with, even if the speaker is qualified to discuss it. The problem is compounded if the speaker is not qualified to do so, as is the case of many who ascend the pulpits without prior religious knowledge from true centers of knowledge and instead depend solely on general religious information. Preachers should not use the pulpit as a means to spread personal opinions that provoke differences and disagreements between religious people. Whoever takes this path in preaching and speaking should not be trusted or relied on by the believers for the religious upbringing of their children.

---

190. 27 Dhul-Hijjah 1440 AH. Statement Regarding Muharram 1441. Source: [https://www.sistani.org/arabic/archive/26341]

Instead, they should turn to the trusted, righteous, and pious scholars.[191]

Pearl 88: Precision in relaying the Holy Quran and Hadith

It is necessary to be precise when stating Quranic verses and narrating noble narrations from the authentic books, or when describing confirmed historical events because a lack of accuracy deteriorates the audience's trust in the Hussaini pulpit.[192] It is important for the speaker to rely on trusted sources for what they convey in their lectures, especially when narrating events that transpired regarding the family of Prophet Muhammad (pbuh&hp), because this reinforces faith in the believers. Moreover, they should avoid questionable or untrustworthy sources so that it cannot be used to invalidate the point being made or one of its most important benefits.[193]

Pearl 89: Being mindful of what is delivered

Preachers must be thoughtful in the content they deliver, and its interpretation, premises and subtleties. A wise speaker is careful in their speech and pays attention to these details. One may deliver a speech,

---

191. 9 Jumada al-Akhir 1440 AH, Fatwa. Source:
[https://www.sistani.org/arabic/archive/26261]

192. 23 Dhul-Hijjah 1437 AH. Advice for Speakers and Preachers Regarding the month of Muharram 1438. Source:
[https://www.sistani.org/arabic/archive/25463]

193. 5 Muharram 1438 AH, Friday Sermon. Source:
[https://www.sistani.org/arabic/archive/25477]

but people may understand something other than what was meant, they may point out an explanation or goal unintentionally, what they say may have an effect which they did not expect, or someone may twist its meaning with bad intention and defame them and confuse the truth. These circumstances are very possible in this time because recording devices and cameras are available and accessible. Therefore, one must be careful in what they say, even in a private environment, because it can be exposed and circulated. Thus, they should speak in a manner that is appropriate for the place because every place has a suitable discourse and every discourse has a suitable place. Speakers and poets do not truly embody that role if they do not consider all aspects of their speech or poetry, respectively, and control every aspect of its development in an appropriate manner such that it prevents pitfalls and confusion, which should always be avoided.[194] It is important for the speaker to have high standards of awareness, alertness, and caution in every word they speak and ensure that they do not say anything inadvertently. This means that they must not only have good intentions in their actions, consider the consequences, and suitably prepare to execute it, but also show true sincerity in opening their minds and doing their best to understand what they are presenting to the affirm wisdom and improve results. Thus, the speaker prepares in a way that is required and does not speak against their will, and take into account their own experiences and the experiences of others. It has been narrated that, "A believer acutely

---

194. 27 Dhul-Hijjah 1440 AH. Statement Regarding Muharram 1441. Source: [https://www.sistani.org/arabic/archive/26341]

assesses and acts decisively"[195] and, "they see with the light of Allah Almighty"[196] and, "they are not stung by the same source twice,"[197] and, "the tongue of a reasoning person is behind their heart, and the heart of a fool is behind their tongue."[198] They perform good deeds while being full of cognizance of God, "And those who give what they give while their hearts are full of fear that they must return unto their Lord. These (are they who) hasten in good things and they are the foremost to (attain) them."[199] Thus, "He grants wisdom to whom He wills, and whoever has been granted wisdom, indeed has been given abundant good, yet no one will mind but the possessors of intellects."[200] [201]

Pearl 90: Precision in presenting the truth

Preachers, poets, and reciters should be very careful in presenting the truth without exaggeration in the matter of the Prophet and his family. There are two kinds of exaggeration: attributing divine qualities to other than God and affirming matters that do not have reliable proof to support them. The school of Ahl al-Bayt (p) does not have either kinds of exaggeration, in

---

195. Al-Reyshahri, Mizan al-Hikma, vol.1, p.208.

196. Al-Majlisi, Bihar al-Anwar, vol.43, p.8.

197. Ibn Abi al-Hadid, Commentary on Nahj al-Balaghah, vol.15, p.45.

198. Al-Majlisi, Bihar al-Anwar, vol.1, p.159.

199. The Holy Quran, 23:60-61

200. The Holy Quran, 2:269.

201. 27 Dhul-Hijjah 1440 AH. Statement Regarding Muharram 1441. Source: [https://www.sistani.org/arabic/archive/26341]

fact it is the furthest away from it. It displays the merits of the Prophet and Ahl al-Bayt (p) in the positions that God Almighty placed them without any embellishment or excess. Instead, it is careful about not affirming anything that is suspicious and questionable, and anything that is not proven and trustworthy. A truly pious person does not exaggerate about the ones they love just as they do not unjustly treat the ones they despise. It is not appropriate to establish religious meanings based solely on love, and to believe anyone who contributes any unverified facts or accept it as part of faith because this leads to innovation in religion without proof, heresy, greed of those who are ignorant, leadership of the people of misguidance, and the withdrawal of pious people who work on the basis of proof and do not accept suspicions. All of this destroys religion and results in an effect that is opposite of the negligence by others. Adding to the faith without reliable evidence is like lessening what has been established with proof. Whoever adds something today without proof will notice that tomorrow more will be added to it, until they are accused of willful negligence and passivity. Therefore, necessitating proof and proper measure is more praiseworthy and safe.[202]

Pearl 91: The sanctity and lofty position of majalis

Preachers should avoid styles and approaches that are not appropriate for the majalis of God, His Messenger, and his successors because the subject matter requires appropriate manners and decorum; violating it would

---

202. Ibid.

violate its objective and change its identity. Perhaps it may even be considered insulting and disrespectful.[203]

Pearl 92: Considering the impact of educational speeches on the community

Preachers should be careful to ensure the correctness of the content of their speeches and their educational effects on the audience and community, just as they are careful while speaking to their families and children. A meaning may be correct and a behavior may be permissible, but its mention and practice should be avoided because it is not appropriate in terms of the effect it has on the minds of the audience. The duty of the callers to God Almighty is to simultaneously remind and provide a means for improvement.[204]

Pearl 93: Examining the past and present

One of the factors that helps increase the understanding of the preacher in what they deliver to the audience is studying history and modern events. This includes incidences that require criticism, disavowal, promotion, and clarification because all of that represents an indispensable experience which one should study. This increases awareness and brings attention to aspects that require caution and may be a source of division.[205]

---

203. Ibid.

204. Ibid.

205. Ibid.

Pearl 94: A speech's engagement with the general public and its attraction

Part of the speaker's skill and creativity is displayed through their choice of the most appropriate examples of the legacy of Ahl al-Bayt (p), all of which are beautiful and great. However, their true mastery is displayed through their choice of verses and narrations which attract all people, regardless of their different religions and social and intellectual inclinations. This follows the approach narrated by Imam Rida (p), "Indeed, if people knew the impact of our words, they would follow us."[206] The beauty of their words is their heritage, which displays humane values that attract all people regardless of their religious and cultural views.[207]

Pearl 95: Not repelling people

Preachers must be careful of phrasing their speech in a way that does not repel people, like generalizing statements of criticism and finding fault with the audience. If they criticize something, they should specify it and not generalize, and if possible, it is better to just reproach rather than [harshly] criticize. They should also take into consideration the good traits and proper practices of others, so that it can be a form of encouragement and a positive acknowledgment of its

---

206. Al-Saduq, Uyoun Akhbar al-Redha (p), vol.2, p.275.

207. 23 Dhul-Hijjah 1437 AH. Advice for Speakers and Preachers Regarding the month of Muharram 1438. Source: [https://www.sistani.org/arabic/archive/25463]

doers.[208] Preachers, as well as the organizers of majalis and processions, should avoid contradiction, hate, division, and difference, especially if they are in a non-Islamic country because that undermines sincerity, decreases the reward, and causes distrust between the believers, which leads to the disruption of initiates that require cooperation and unity to complete. Anyone who can keep their work and contributions secret, like a secret charity, without seeking control, fame, or status, should. As God Almighty said, "If you give alms openly, it is well, but if you hide it and give it to the poor, it is better for you, and it will remove from you some of your sins, and Allah is aware of what you do."[209] He also said, "And whosoever fears Allah, He will make a way for him to get out from all hardships. And He will provide him from sources unimaginable to him. And whosoever puts his trust in Allah, then He will suffice him. Verily, Allah will accomplish his purpose. Indeed Allah has set a measure for all things."[210] [211]

Pearl 96: Reminding of the important and common jurisprudential issues

It is recommended for speakers to discuss the important and common jurisprudential issues, especially

208. 27 Dhul-Hijjah 1440 AH. Statement Regarding Muharram 1441. Source: [https://www.sistani.org/arabic/archive/26341]

209. The Holy Quran, 2:271.

210. The Holy Quran, 65:2-3.

211. 27 Dhul-Hijjah 1440 AH. Statement Regarding Muharram 1441. Source: [https://www.sistani.org/arabic/archive/26341]

contemporary matters of worship and transactions, in an interesting and clear manner that makes the audience feel that the Hussaini pulpit is connected to reality and their different circumstances.[212]

Pearl 97: Refuting commonly encountered suspicions

It is obvious that one of the clearest examples of preserving the religion and strengthening it in our modern era by refuting commonly encountered suspicions about it, its fundamentals, and its moral values. However, it is necessary to consider the following issue in this regard:

1. Speakers who are devoted to refuting suspicions about religion should be experienced to do so and armed with virtue and an abundance of knowledge. Otherwise, they might corrupt more than repair. The pulpit is one of the most important means to refute the suspicions against the true faith. The Prophet and the Commander of the Faithful refuted the doubts that were raised in the minds of some Muslims due to their adherence to ignorant (pre-Islamic era) principles or the influence of non-Islamic communities, in addition to explaining the nature of knowledge and religious teachings. This is because the Hussaini pulpit is of great importance and an extension of the message of the

---

212. 23 Dhul-Hijjah 1437 AH. Advice for Speakers and Preachers Regarding the month of Muharram 1438. Source: [https://www.sistani.org/arabic/archive/25463]

Prophet and Imam Ali (p). Thus, the person who ascends it should be qualified and knowledgeable.

2. There are two kinds of suspicions, some are common and popularly held, while others are raised sometimes but are not too common. It is appropriate, rather, it is necessary to be committed to directly refuting the suspicions that are common in the public. However, it is not suitable to mention rare suspicions in public. Instead, one must correctly solve them in a clear way so they are removed from the minds of the few people who harbor them without having to overtly mention or refer to them.

3. It is known that every situation has a suitable discourse. Therefore, preachers should be aware of the intellectual and cultural level of the audience, either directly or through indirect means. Thus, they should not discuss religious matters that do not suit the intellectual level of the audience. They should be careful when describing suspicious issues and clarifying the answer in proportion to impact the minds of the listeners. It has been narrated that the great Messenger said, "We the Prophets have been commanded to speak to people in proportion to their minds."213

4. It is important to exert every effort possible to spread the knowledge of Ahl al-Bayt (p) which has been narrated through trusted and reliable sources. It has been narrated that Imam Rida (p) said, "Indeed, if people knew the impact of our words, they would

---

213. Al-Kulayni, al-Kafi, vol.1, p.23.

follow us."[214] The beauty of their words include a complete intellectual system that encompasses diverse content like the Holy Quran. It has marvels of wisdom, moral standards, stimuli for dormant minds, and refutation of suspicions, which enlighten Muslims and makes them more confident in their faith and religion. This is because the Ahl al-Bayt (p) are the second weighty thing along with the Quran as clearly stated in the narration of the two weighty things and other similar traditions. Hussaini speakers should care about this aspect of their speech like they give attention to mentioning the sufferings of Ahl al-Bayt (p) and what happened in the tragedy of Karbala because this is a great way to keep this matter alive in the minds.[215]

Pearl 98: To not weaken or permit emboldening

Preachers should be careful when explaining the importance of the true doctrines of faith and the doctrine of the Ahl al-Bayt (p) in demonstrating their holy position and from weakening the significance of obedience and trivializing disobedience in the eyes of people. The affairs of a believer cannot be set aright without fear and hope. Therefore, they must maintain a balance between them personally and in the matter of others. There is no immunity in religion for anyone who sins, except the rare and small sins that a person may commit occasionally and then awakens and

---

214. Al-Saduq, Uyoun Akhbar al-Redha (p), vol.2, p.275.

215. 11 Dhul-Hijjah 1439 AH. Advice for Speakers and Preachers Regarding the month of Muharram 1440. Source: [https://www.sistani.org/arabic/archive/26110]

repents to God Almighty. Poignant preachers should not assure anyone safety from God's punishment when they sin, nor should they give them reason to despair from hope in Him and His pardon, and the intercession of His vicegerents with His permission, as long as they sincerely repent to Him. They must remember and remind of His saying, "and called upon Us in yearning and awe,"[216] "... that man can have nothing but what he strives for, and that his deeds will be seen, then he will be recompensed with a full and the best recompense,"[217] and, "It is not your vain desires, nor the vain desires of the people of the Book. Whoever does evil shall be recompensed for it and besides Allah, he will find for himself neither a guardian nor a helper,"[218] along with the many noble narrations as well.[219]

Pearl 99: Setting a standard of high quality

One of the factors that affects delivery and its impact on the audience is the quality of preparation. This means that the speaker should completely care about what they discuss of topics in terms of arrangement, categorization, and clear and smooth exposition. In addition, they should choose expressions and manners that appeal to the audience and viewers, exerting great effort in preparing the topics, organizing them, and displaying them in a clear and appealing manner,

---

216. The Holy Quran, 21:90.

217. The Holy Quran, 53:39-41

218. The Holy Quran, 4:123

219. 27 Dhul-Hijjah 1440 AH. Statement Regarding Muharram 1441. Source: [https://www.sistani.org/arabic/archive/26341]

which will contribute to the interaction of the audience with the Hussaini pulpit.[220]

Pearl 100: Appropriate qualities and self-discipline

Preachers should display the appropriate qualities and manners for this noble position. Every job has suitable characteristics in terms of appearance, and general and unique behaviors. Preaching and performing Hussaini elegies also have appropriate qualities that should accompany the content, which covers speaking about the truth, the Imams of guidance, and all that is required of righteousness and vigilance. This is achieved by embodying the elements of dignity, like not prioritizing money and avoiding anything that causes misunderstandings and promotes covetousness. One should observe chastity in all worldly goals to fulfill this role.[221] Preachers should question themselves, thus purifying their sayings and actions, understanding that they are not safe from wrongdoings and remembering God Almighty and His supervision over Him while preaching and in all other states. Moreover, they should know that they will be asked on the Day of Judgement, having benefitted from others' criticism of

---

220. 23 Dhul-Hijjah 1437 AH. Advice for Speakers and Preachers Regarding the month of Muharram 1438. Source: [https://www.sistani.org/arabic/archive/25463]

221. 27 Dhul-Hijjah 1440 AH. Statement Regarding Muharram 1441. Source: [https://www.sistani.org/arabic/archive/26341]

them and thus reforming themselves and responding to the call of the truth.[222]

---

222. Ibid.

Appendix

A Biography of His Eminence
Sayyid al-Sistani

Birth and Lineage

His Eminence Sayyid al-Sistani was born on the ninth of Rabi al-Awwal in 1439 AH in the Holy City of Mashhad in Iran.[223]

His father is Sayyid Muhammad Baqir, the son of Sayyid Ali al-Husayni al-Sistani (may God have mercy on them). Both were prominent and well-known scholars in the religious seminaries in Najaf, Qum, and Mashhad.

His lineage is traced to Imam Hussain ibn Ali ibn Abi Talib (p) (may peace be upon them), the son of Fatimah, daughter of Muhammad (pbuh&hp) (may God's blessings be upon them and their progeny).

---

223. Most of the information herein was taken from the official website of the office of His Eminence, www.sistani.org, with some additions and alterations.

Character

Most of the people who have known His Eminence Sayyid al-Sistani and have accompanied him have noted that, since his youth, he was a quiet person who spent most of his time in meditation and reflection. They say he has a calm, content, and patient personality. He is very humble and has lived an extremely simple life. His asceticism is apparent from his food, clothing, and residence. He does not like dissemblance and forbids his representatives from spending a penny on advertising his religious authority or posting his pictures in public places. Moreover, he does not like titles, to the extent that he has deleted the title of "Ayatullah" from some pages of his office's website. Also, he does not allow any organization or Islamic center to be named after him. Instead, he instructs believers to name them after historic scholars in order to resurrect their names and keep them in memory. Finally, there is his fatherly spirit. He does not favor a person over another, whatever their color, language, ethnicity, or status. He considers himself a father to all believers—needing to be fair and just in treating them all.

Scholarly Journey

His Eminence started learning the Quran and reading and writing at the age of five years. He started studying religious disciplines by the beginning of the second decade of his life and continued until he attended the doctrinal lectures of Ayatullah Mirza Mahdi al-Ashtiani and the jurisprudential research lectures of Ayatullah Mirza Hashim al-Qazwini in Mashhad.

He moved to the religious seminary in Qum in 1368 AH and attended the research lectures of the supreme religious authority, Sayyid Hussain al-Tabatabai al-Burujirdi (may God have mercy on him), on jurisprudence and its roots. He also learned much about the disciplines of hadith and biographical evaluation from him. In addition, he attended the lectures of the great jurisprudent, Sayyid Muhammad al-Hujjah al-Kuhkamari (may God have mercy on him).

He decamped to the religious seminary in Najaf at the beginning of the year 1371 AH and has resided there ever since. He attended the research lectures on jurisprudence and its roots given by the two prominent figures Sayyid Abu al-Qasim al-Musawi al-Khui and Shaykh Hussain al-Hilli (may God have mercy on them) and accompanied them for a long period of time. During that time, he also attended the research lectures of other prominent figures including Sayyid Muhsin al-Hakim and Sayyid Mahmud al-Shahrudi (may God have mercy on them).

He outshined his peers through wit, ample research, perseverance in learning, and familiarity with various theories in different religious disciplines, thereby becoming in 1381 AH the only one among his peers (i.e., the scholars in the early thirties) to receive the following certificates from prominent scholars:

- Certificate of absolute ijtihad from his master, His Eminence Sayyid al-Khui (may God have mercy on him), who did not give such a certificate to anyone except him and Shaykh Ali al-Falsafi

- Certificate of absolute ijtihad from his master, Shaykh Hussain al-Hilli, who did not issue such a certificate to anyone other than His Eminence
- A certificate from the greatest of muhaddiths, Shaykh Agha Buzurg al-Tehrani, commending His Eminence's skill in the disciplines of hadith and biographical evaluation. The certificate was dated 1380 AH.

He taught jurisprudential research beginning in 1381 AH and roots of jurisprudence research beginning in 1384 AH. However, deteriorating security conditions have compelled him to stop lecturing in recent years.

He has authored more than forty published and unpublished works. A complete list of them can be found on the website of His Eminence's office, may God prolong his life.

Features of His Eminence's School of Thought

His Eminence cares about knowing the roots of the jurisprudential question and its surrounding circumstances, including the doctrinal and political environment, before issuing his jurisprudential verdict. Thus, he does not limit himself to religious texts only.

He connects seminary thought to contemporary culture. The reason is that a question may take many manifestations, requiring the jurisprudent to know all the schools of thought and what makes them have different opinions and interpretations of the same issue.

He is committed to the principle of modernization in the theories and premises of jurisprudence and its roots and does not settle for discussing the existing literature and commenting on it. Take the principle of respect as an example. It is the principle of respecting others and their opinions and laws. His Eminence modernized this great Islamic principle and formulated it as a jurisprudential code used by believers who live in non-Muslim or mixed, multi-religious countries.

He is committed to the comparative study of the different schools of great religious seminaries, using the opinions of their most prominent jurisprudents. For example, he mentions the opinion of Sayyid al-Burujirdi as a representative of the school of Qum; then he mentions the opinions of Sayyid al-Khui and Shaykh Hussain al-Hilli as representatives of the school of Najaf; then he compares and analyzes those opinions before finally giving his own opinion. He does the same when discussing issues in which the jurisprudents of the Shia Imami school have a different opinion than that of the jurisprudents of other Islamic schools.

He is thoroughly aware of other disciplines and specialties, such as contemporary law. For example, he examines French, Egyptian, and Iraqi laws and employs them in analyzing jurisprudential principles and expanding their use.

Religious Authority

His Eminence was among the most distinguished students of the Supreme Religious Authority, Sayyid al-Khui (may God have mercy on him) (1413 AH), as he was the only one of his students to give research lectures during his life. His master paid special attention to his abilities and even appointed him to be the imam of congregational prayer at al-Khadra Mosque.[224] After the passing away of Sayyid al-Khui, Sayyid al-Gulpaygani (may God have mercy on him) of Qum and Sayyid Abd al-Ala al-Sabzawari (may God have mercy on him) of Najaf emerged as religious authorities. However, both of them passed away shortly (1414 AH). After them, Shaykh Muhammad Ali al-Araki and Sayyid Muhammad al-Ruhani (may God have mercy on them) emerged as religious authorities. Nevertheless, they passed away in a short period of time too. Consequently, people in religious and seminary circles looked upon His Eminence Sayyid al-Sistani (may God prolong his life) because of his high religious stature and his piety and prudence. Several prominent jurisprudents, such as His Eminence Ayatullah Sayyid Ali al-Bihishti and His Eminence Ayatullah Murtada al-Burujirdi in addition to many senior lecturers in the seminaries of Qum and Najaf, directed believers to emulate Sayyid al-Sistani. As a result, many believers in Iraq, Iran, the Gulf, Pakistan, and India started to emulate His Eminence. Soon, most believers in other Muslim and non-Muslim countries around the world were emulating him. To this day, he is the supreme religious authority who has the most emulators among believers.

---

224. Al-Khadra Mosque is a historical mosque adjacent to the shrine of the Leader of the Faithful, may peace be upon him. It has a high symbolic status. For years, only supreme religious authorities led congregational prayers in it and lectured there.

May the Almighty prolong his life and help Islam and Muslims with his existence.

Struggle and Important Events

His Eminence resisted the plan of the Baathist regime to suppress the religious seminary with the highest degree of patience and forbearance. The Baathist regime expelled many jurisprudents and scholars, including some of His Eminence Sayyid al-Sistani's students. His Eminence himself was on the verge of being expelled several times. He was questioned more than once and tolerated the insults and offenses of the Baathists. However, all that pressure could not change his decision not to leave the religious seminary in Najaf.

He tolerated and resisted the pressure and harassment of the Baathist regime during the Iran-Iraq war. When Iraqi people revolted in 1411 AH and the regime crushed the revolution with brute force, it detained His Eminence Sayyid al-Sistani and many other scholars. They were persecuted, harshly questioned, and even tortured in the notorious Ridhwaniyah detention camp. The Baathist regime later assassinated some of them such as Martyr Ayatullah Shaykh Murtada al-Burujirdi and Martyr Ayatullah Mirza Ali al-Gharawi.

After the passing away of the Supreme Religious Authority Sayyid al-Khui (may God be pleased with him) and the acceptance of His Eminence Sayyid al-Sistani as a religious authority, the Baathist regime pressed to change the direction of the religious authority in Najaf. It did what it could to tarnish the reputation of Sayyid al-Sistani and damage his stature among jurisprudents and used various methods to not let believers meet him, such as closing al-Khadra Mosque in 1414 AH. When all those attempts failed, the regime planned to assassinate him, as documents recovered after the fall of the Baath regime show.[225] As a result, he stayed in his house for several years and could not even visit the shrine of the Leader of the Faithful (may peace be upon him) although his house was only a few meters from the shrine.

After the fall of the Baathist regime and the occupation of Iraq in 1424 AH (2003 CE), the occupiers attempted to dictate a certain constitution and system of government to Iraqis. In response, His Eminence Sayyid al-Sistani (may God prolong his life) sent a letter to the Security Council warning of the risks of approving the so-called transitional law. The Security Council complied with the request of His Eminence. Also, he issued his famous edict insisting that only Iraqis draft the new constitution, that there be a referendum on the constitution so that Iraqis decide whether or not it takes effect, and that the constitution not be in conflict with Islamic principles and the noble values of the Iraqi people.[226] In the end, that was what happened, and the system of government in the new Iraq was in compliance with the opinion of the supreme religious authority, embodied in His

225. "The Hawza under Siege," by Dr. Abbas Kadhim, Boston University. Online PDF file available on: http://www.bu.edu/iis/files/2013/04/ Bath-Party-ArchiveFinal-1.pdf

226. The edict can be found on the website of the office of His Eminence Sayyid al-Sistani: http://www.sistani.org/arabic/archive/273/

Appendix

Eminence Grand Ayatullah Sayyid al-Sistani (may God prolong his life). Therefore, he not only protected Iraq from being dominated by the occupiers but contributed to protecting the entire region from a grand plan for which the occupation of Iraq was only the beginning.

His Eminence Sayyid al-Sistani left Iraq on the nineteenth of Shaban 1425 AH (August 6, 2004) to have a heart surgery in one of London's hospitals. His absence encouraged various local and foreign parties to exploit the resulting power vacuum and its psychological effects on the political situation. As a result, violence broke out in Iraq and warring factions entered even the holy shrine of Imam Ali (may peace be upon him) and used it as a base. This exposed Najaf to shelling and destruction and the holy shrine was on the verge of being destroyed. At that time, the medical authorities in the British hospital permitted His Eminence to leave the hospital. He immediately left and boarded the first plane going to Kuwait. Upon landing in Kuwait, he headed directly to Basra. Then he joined millions of believers in a grand march from Basra to Najaf. Despite all the risks and the possibility of a disaster threatened by some parties in the war, His Eminence (may God prolong his life) insisted on liberating Najaf from warfare, whatever the price. His Eminence arrived in Najaf with millions accompanying him on the ninth of Rajab. Upon seeing millions marching toward them, the warring parties left the holy shrine. As such, His Eminence prevented a catastrophe that would have irreparably damaged the dignity and status of the Imami school of Islam.

As a result of the fall of the Baathist regime and the occupation, Iraq witnessed unusual waves of politicized sectarian fighting. Frantic campaigns of identity-based killing started. Leaders of aberration, along with commanders of some factions, helped this sectarian unrest with funds, weapons, and propaganda until it reached such a high degree that the holy shrine of the two Askari imams in Samarra was detonated on the twenty-third of Muharram 1427 AH. The entire country was on the verge of explosion, and the Tigris and Euphrates rivers were at risk of being colored red with blood. His Eminence employed his wisdom and shrewdness and the highest degree of restraint despite all the tragedies and atrocities he was witnessing. He issued religious edicts and instructions to forbid assaulting any human being, whether they be Muslim or non-Muslim, a Shia or a Sunni. He repeated his famous saying, "Do not say, 'Our brothers, the Sunnis,' but say, 'Ourselves.'" He forbade seizing the mosques of one sect by another and pressured zealots to leave the mosques they had seized although those mosques were in their areas. As such, he was able to stop the sectarian war and return peace and security to Iraq and its people. However, it should be noted that attempts to reignite sectarian war in Iraq have not stopped.

Last but not least is the historical religious edict of collective jihad[227] on the eleventh of Shaban 1435 AH against the terrorist group ISIS, which crossed the border overnight and occupied Mosul and reached as

227. The edict can be found on the website of the office of His Eminence Sayyid al-Sistani:
http://www.sistani.org/arabic/statement/24906/

far as a few kilometers from Baghdad amid a complete collapse of the Iraqi army and high treason by its leadership in the area. Immediately, thousands of believers volunteered to become soldiers under the command of the Iraqi army, obeying the order issued by His Eminence (may God prolong his life) as he refused to let them fight under the command of any entity except the official Iraqi army. This religious edict was a first, coming approximately 100 years after the edict of jihad against the British occupiers of Iraq in 1920 CE. As a result, Iraq and the region were prevented from falling under the control of the Khawarij of our time and the leaders of aberration. We ask God, the Glorified, to protect believers and their homelands from the evil of their enemies embodied in al-Qaeda, Taliban, ISIS, the Nusra, and other groups and to expedite the return of our master, Imam al-Mahdi (may peace be upon him), who will spread justice and equity in this world after it is filled with injustice and inequity.

His Eminence Sayyid al-Sistani is the first religious authority to be commended by the Security Council of the United Nations for his role in combating terrorism and his sponsorship of displaced Sunni Muslims, Christians, and other minorities who sought refuge in Najaf and Karbala after the brutal assault of the terrorists ISIS. The commendation was announced in the Security Council report issued on January 10, 2014.[228] His Eminence is also the first religious authority visited in his residence by the Secretary-General of the United Nations, Ban Ki-Moon, who thanked him for his efforts

---

228. http://www.un.org/apps/news/story.asp?NewsID=46909&Cr= Iraq&Cr1=#.VwigrEfko1p

and position against extremism and terror. The visit took place for about one hour on July 24, 2014. The Secretary-General expressed his appreciation for Sayyid al-Sistani and his call for peace and preserving the unity of the country. He said, "I am extremely honored to have met His Eminence Grand Ayatollah Al-Sistani today for the first time. He is a man of the deepest wisdom and tolerance. He is an inspiration and a role model for his many followers in Iraq and beyond." He added, "I expressed the United Nations' gratitude for His Eminence's support for all efforts to protect civilians in the current conflict...I expressed to His Eminence how deeply moved I was by his consistent calls for all sides to refrain from sectarian or ethnic rhetoric." The Secretary-General ended his remarks by saying, "Once again, I was deeply impressed by my time with His Eminence. You can continue to count on my full support along with the United Nations as the people of Najaf and all of Iraq work to build a tolerant, peaceful, and prosperous country for all its people."[229]

Similarly, His Eminence Sayyid al-Sistani is the first religious authority in the Islamic world to be visited in his humble residence in the holy city of Najaf by a great religious personality like His Holiness Pope Francis (Jorge Mario Bergoglio), who is the 266th pope of the Catholic Church. The meeting took place on the 6th of May 2021 during the pope's historical visit to Iraq to support minorities and promote peace. It was an exceptionally significant and spiritual meeting which had broad international support and a positive and fruitful outcome. The pope was impressed and moved

---

229. http://www.un.org/sg/offthecuff/index.asp?nid=3496

by the personality of Sayyid al-Sistani, his conversation, and his humble residence. He described Sayyid al-Sistani as, "the wise" and "man of God."[230] Moreover, the Vatican's official statement described the visit, "The meeting was an occasion for the Pope to thank Grand Ayatollah al-Sistani for speaking up (together with the Shia community) in defense of those most vulnerable and persecuted amid the violence and great hardships of recent years, and for affirming the sanctity of human life and the importance of the unity of the Iraqi people."[231]

Similarly, the office of Sayyid al-Sistani in the holy city of Najaf announced that His Eminence and the Pope of the Vatican discussed the great challenges which humanity is facing in this era, the role of faith in God Almighty and His message, and commitment and adherence to moral duties in overcoming the challenges.

His Eminence Sayyid al-Sistani spoke about the suffering of many people in various countries dealing with injustice, oppression, poverty, religious and intellectual persecution, suppression of fundamental freedoms, and the absence of social equity. His Eminence pointed out the critical role prominent religious leadership must play in limiting these tragedies, and the importance of fostering and coordinating efforts to strengthen the values of harmony, peaceful coexistence, and human solidarity in all communities based on the protection of

[230] https://www.vaticannews.va/en/pope/news/2021-03/pope-francis-inflight-presser-iraq-journalists0.html

[231] https://www.vaticannews.va/en/pope/news/2021-03/pope-francis-stresses-importance-of-cooperation-fraternity-in-m.html

rights and mutual respect between followers of different religions and intellectual opinions.

His Eminence also praised Iraq, its glorious history, and the merits of its noble people in all their diverse ethnicities. He expressed hope that it will overcome its current suffering soon. He affirmed his concern for the Christian citizens and expressed that they should live like all other Iraqis in safety and peace and with all their constitutional rights. He also referred to the role of the religious authority in protecting them and all those who are affected by oppression and suffering in the events of the past years, especially during the period when terrorists controlled vast areas of Iraqi provinces and practiced heinous criminal acts which are decried by all people.[232]

---

[232] https://www.sistani.org/arabic/statement/26506/

Other publications from I.M.A.M.

Available for purchase online

- ❖ Advice to Youth
  By Grand Ayatullah Sayyid Ali al-Sistani

- ❖ Fasting: A Haven from Hellfire
  by Grand Ayatullah Sayyid Ali al-Sistani

- ❖ God's Emissaries: Adam to Jesus
  by Shaykh Rizwan Arastu

- ❖ Islam and Christianity: Brothers at Odds
  by Odeh Muhawesh

- ❖ Islamic Laws
  by Grand Ayatullah Sayyid Ali al-Sistani

- ❖ Islamic Laws of Expiations
  by Grand Ayatullah Sayyid Ali al-Sistani

- ❖ Islamic Laws of Death and Burial
  by Grand Ayatullah Sayyid Ali al-Sistani

- ❖ Islamic Laws of Food and Drink
  by Grand Ayatullah Sayyid Ali al-Sistani

- ❖ Who Is Hussain?
  by Dr. Mehdi Saeed Hazari

- ❖ Shia Muslims: Our Identity, Our Vision, and
  the Way Forward by Sayyid M. B. Kashmiri

- ❖ Tajwid: A Guide to Qur'anic Recitation
  by Shaykh Rizwan Arastu

- ❖ The Illuminating Lantern: An Exposition of
  Subtleties from the Quran
  by Shaykh Habib al-Kadhimi

Printed in Great Britain
by Amazon